AMERICAN POETS PROJECT

IS PUBLISHED WITH A GIFT IN MEMORY OF

James Merrill

AND SUPPORT FROM ITS FOUNDING PATRONS

Sidney J. Weinberg, Jr. Foundation

The Berkley Foundation

Richard B. Fisher and Jeanne Donovan Fisher

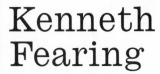

Kenneth Fearing

selected poems

robert polito editor

AMERICAN POETS PROJECT

THE LIBRARY OF AMERICA

Design by Chip Kidd and Mark Melnick.
Frontispiece courtesy of The Estate of Kenneth Fearing.

Library of Congress Cataloging-in-Publication Data:
Fearing, Kenneth, 1902–1961.
    [Poems. Selections]
    Selected poems / Kenneth Fearing ; Robert Polito, editor.
       p. cm. — (American poets project ; 8)
       Includes index.
       ISBN 1–931082–57–X (alk. paper)
       I. Polito, Robert. II. Title. III. Series.
    PS3511.E115A6 2004
    2003060482

10 9 8 7 6 5 4 3 2 1

Kenneth
Fearing

CONTENTS

INTRODUCTION

What will you do . . .
Do with the culture found in a tabloid, what can be done with a
    Lydia Pinkham ad?

                —Kenneth Fearing, "As the Fuse Burns Down"

The tags that tend to cluster around his name signal caveat as well as homage—a "depression poet" (M. L. Rosenthal), a "poet for workers" (Edward Dahlberg), a poet who "thought . . . like a taxi driver reading a billboard while fighting traffic" (Kenneth Rexroth)—yet Kenneth Fearing's poems carry no whiff of the curio or relic. If anything, his poems of the 1920s and 30s impress through their canniness—particularly regarding the incipient culture industry of film, radio, television, newspapers, gossip —and prescience. Fearing insinuated an emerging media universe poetry still only fitfully acknowledges. No one would claim that most contemporary poets exactly inhabit the same psychic or epistemological landscape as Tennyson; but how rarely does our poetry calculate the saturation of "the new and complex harmonies, it seems, of a strange and still more complex age," as Fearing described the new media in his poem "Reception Good." Many poets might be prompted to invoke romantic love via an advertising slogan, as Fearing does in "Aphrodite Metropolis," but the culture industry usually is summoned even now to poems for irony or decoration, often with an aim of securing emotional truths viewed as beyond (and more profound than) any mass-culture representations.

Born near the start of the Edison-Hearst-Disney century, Fearing posited no irreducible alternatives to his media-steeped snapshots of desire, profit, despair, violence, and death. Consider—speaking of Tennyson and, still more opportunely, Keats—the poem Fearing positioned at the head of his first book, *Angel Arms* (1929), "St. Agnes' Eve," with its bravura lead-in:

The dramatis personæ include a fly-specked Monday
        evening,
    A cigar store with stagnant windows,
    Two crooked streets,
    Six policemen and Louie Glatz.
Bass drums mumble and mutter an ominous portent
    As Louie Glatz holds up the cigar store and backs out
        with
$14.92.

Along with Stevens' *Harmonium* (1923) and Moore's *Observations* (1924), *Angel Arms* secured one of the iconic modernist debuts of the American 1920s, and "St. Agnes' Eve" is his sly calling card for the new poetry. Instead of Keats' drowsy Spenserian erotics, Fearing's gritty free-verse modifiers—"fly-specked," "stagnant," and "crooked"

—usher in a brutal city shootout, even as the opening ("The dramatis personæ include . . .") lodges a droll theatricality and the screenplay ending ("Close-up . . . Picture . . . fade out slow") intimates the poem already is a film. Glatz's antic exit—"'I'm not shot,' he screamed, / 'it isn't me they've shot in the head,' he laughed, 'Oh / I don't give a damn!'"—anticipates by more than twenty years James Cagney (as Cody Jarrett) in Raoul Walsh's *White Heat* howling "on top of the world" from an exploding gas tank. But of course crime movies in 1926, the year "St. Agnes' Eve" appeared in *New Masses*, were silent except for accompanying orchestral soundtracks ("Violins moan . . ."), so the repeated "Rat-a-tat-tat" and "Blam! Blam!-blam!" more likely derive from comic strips. Newspaper locutions ("it is supposed") and pulpy strokes ("stammering syllables of instant death . . . big vacant galleries of night") vie with surreal, Chaplinesque signatures—the dancing derby hat of Louie's departing "soul"—and portentous totems, such as the stolen "$14.92," also the date of Columbus' original New World stick-up. Yet even scattered "poetic" flourishes —"Space curls its arm across the flat roofs"—ultimately fragment into words overheard from other poems: Robinson, or Sandburg, maybe, by way of Eliot. Every action, emotion, and the various "dramatis personæ" in the poem arrive embedded inside a diction, a medium, the offhand dash of "St. Agnes' Eve" aligning a scramble of deadpan appropriations.

Angel Arms is conspicuously a book of collages, vitalized and sustained by Fearing's vernacular mastery. The magnificent "Jack Knuckles Falters But Reads Own Statement at His Execution While Wardens Watch" mixes newspaper headlines and the last (or is it posthumous?) testament of a convicted murderer:

Has little to say.
Gentleman, I feel there is little I
　　care to say at this moment, but the press has urged me
　　to express a few appropriate
Thanks Warden for kindness
　　remarks. I
　　am grateful to Warden E. J. Springer for the many
　　kindnesses he has shown me in the last six weeks and I
　　also wish to thank my friends who stuck by me
　　to the last. . . .

Veering from public bulletins to personal avowals of inno-
cence, Fearing resists the obvious tactic of validating
Knuckles' confidentially voiced disclosures over tabloid
distortions. As the condemned man intones his patriotism,

　　. . . As one who entered
　　his nation's defense
Staggers when he sees electric chair
　　five days after war was declared I
　　was hoping for a pardon from the governor,
　　but evidently the government has forgotten its veterans
　　in a moment of need. . . .

or as he elaborates his alibi,

　　What brought me to the chair
　　was keeping bad companions against the advice
　　heard three gun-shots and saw a man running
　　of my mother and companions. . . .

Jack Knuckles sounds at least as tainted and dubious as the
press that is misrepresenting him.

　　Ordinary life rarely enters Fearing's poems except
through the slippery deflections of popular culture, and

there is no snooty distance or criticism, as though for a poet and citizen of the 20th century the inescapable, omnipresent urban media assume roles that the natural world, say, performed for prior poetry. The third section of "Aphrodite Metropolis" recasts Andrew Marvell:

Harry loves Myrtle—He has strong arms
from the warehouse,
and on Sunday when they trolley to emerald meadows
    he doesn't say
"What will your chastity amount to when your flesh
    withers in a little while?"
No,
on Sunday when they trolley to emerald meadows
they look at the Sunday paper
"Girls Slays Banker-Betrayer"
they spread it around on the grass
"Bath-tub Stirs Jersey Row"
and then they sit down on it, nice.
Harry doesn't say "Ziggin's Ointment for withered
    flesh,
cures thousands of men and women of moles, warts,
    red veins,
flabby throat, scalp and hair diseases,
not expensive, and fully guaranteed."
No, Harry says nothing at all,
he smiles,
and they kiss in the emerald meadows on the Sunday
    paper.

For this pastiche of "The Garden" and "To His Coy Mistress," Fearing transforms Marvell's "lovely green" into "emerald meadows," as if quoting an Irish-American travel brochure, and spins the famous caution against sexual coyness first into stilted prose ("What will your chastity amount to . . . ?") and then into a huckster's skin cream pitch ("Ziggin's Ointment for withered flesh . . ."). As the picnicking lovers kiss, headlines from the scandal sheets Harry and Myrtle sit on ("Girl Slays Banker-Betrayer") focus the menace implicit in Marvell's original metaphysical injunction and at the edges of their casual Sunday scene ("He has strong arms / from the warehouse"). Harry may love Myrtle, as the poem says, but who is Harry? Who is Myrtle? For nearly all Fearing's people, their identity, much like their "love," emerges as a medley of voices, a flip-book of images, that twitch inside their brains and ours.

Fearing's subjects are inseparable from the systems—cultural, technological, historical, corporate, stylistic—that have arisen to account for and represent them. His poems are attuned especially to systems of "desire and profit," to quote a bland, almost throwaway line from a minor poem called "Now": "Only desire and profit are real." No other American poet writes so variously (and convincingly) about money, corporations, business, offices, and the transactions of yearning and need. Boardrooms routinely dissolve into bedrooms—"Dividends," for instance, or "X Minus X"—much as in Fassbinder films. His Marxism shaped his second book *Poems* (1935), most visibly in "American Rhapsody (2)," "No Credit," "$2.50," "1933," and "Denouement," but Fearing's innovation is less his anti-capitalism than his alertness to the *sounds* of profit and desire. He evolved a sort of harried, manic prosody that mimics the haywire machinery of runaway capitalism—a nervous, abstract, and relentless music detached from any immediate human agency, any familiar lyric "I." This is the headlong opening of "Dirge":

> 1-2-3 was the number he played but today the number
>   came 3-2-1;
>   bought his Carbide at 30 and it went to 29; had the
>   favorite at Bowie but the track was slow—
>
> O, executive type, would you like to drive a floating
>   power, knee-action, silk upholstered six? Wed a
>   Hollywood star? Shoot the course in 58? Draw to
>   the ace, king, jack?
> O, fellow with a will who won't take no, watch out for
>   three cigarettes on the same, single match; O,
>   democratic voter born in August under Mars,
>   beware of liquidated rails—

Later poems, such as "Hold the Wire" from *Dead Reckoning* (1938), vibrate like that capitalist machinery shaking to pieces:

> If the doorbell rings and we think we were followed
>   here, if the bell should ring but we are not sure
> how can we decide
>
> IF IT'S ONLY THE GASMAN it may be all right,
>   IF HE'S AN AUTHORIZED PERSON IN
>   A DOUBLE-BREASTED SUIT we'd better
>   get it over with, but IF HE'S SOME
>   NOBODY it may be good news
> or it might mean death IF THE SAMPLES ARE FREE

Fearing's demotic lines and serpentine strophes may mark him as a link between William Carlos Williams and Allen Ginsberg, while his furtive collages suggest Lorine Niedecker, and his twilight media dramatic monologues foreshadow Ai. Yet the rhythms of "Dear Beatrice Fairfax"

("Is it true that Father Coughlin and Miss Aimee Semple McPherson and General Hugh Johnson and Mrs. Barbara Mdivani and Mr. Samuel Insull and Miss Greta Garbo and Mr. Prince Mike Romanoff?")—first printed in *New Masses* in 1934—are nothing short of rock 'n' roll, Bob Dylan, or Elvis Costello:

> Foolproof baby with that memorized smile,
>> burglarproof baby, fireproof baby with that rehearsed
>> appeal,
>> reconditioned, standardized, synchronized, amplified,
>> best-by-test baby with those push-the-button
>> tears . . .

Oblique strategies drive and stagger Fearing's work. Amid the constant motion, the constant baffles and refractions, there are no secure vistas, no still points. His poems imply narratives, but without plots, development, even characters. Many, such as "Devil's Dream," "Longshot Blues," and "A Pattern," consist chiefly of questions, slanting and unresolvable. Others, like "Minnie and Mrs. Hoyne," "They Liked It," and "How Do I Feel?" spur cryptic, often sinister and circular dialogues. Some are entirely imperatives—"Conclusion," "Winner Take All," "Resurrection"—that monitor or badger an intangible "you." Fearing's speakers float and shift strophe by strophe, sliding through analogous or contrasting circumstances, as though his poems were equations with fractions and variables. "Green Light" contrives a wondrous maze of inferences, modifications, and reversals:

> Bought at the drug store, very cheap; and later pawned.
>> After a while, heard on the street; seen in the park.
>> Familiar but not quite recognized.
>> Followed and taken home and slept with.
>> Traded or sold. Or lost.
> Bought again at the corner drug store . . .

A void transmits from the core of Fearing's enterprise—"the nothingness that waits and waits," as he wrote in "American Rhapsody (4)." The poems literalize Eliot's remarks on the impersonality of the poet, and traces of someone named "Kenneth Fearing" are nearly impossible to localize. Multifocused and decentered, all his writing frames an elaborate disappearing act. Fearing wrote seven novels, most notably *Dagger of the Mind* (1941), *Clark Gifford's Body* (1942), and *The Big Clock* (1946). Each novel features multiple narrators, and just as in the poems any suspicion of a single controlling intelligence atomizes into a profusion of viewpoints. "HOW DO WE KNOW YOU'RE THE PERSON THAT YOU SAY," he asked in "Hold the Wire." But for both his poetry and fiction, Fearing never did say. The scary "Escape" encodes his—well—his escape:

Acid for the whorls of the fingertips; for the face, a
    surgeon's knife; oblivion to the name;
eyes, hands, color of hair, condition of teeth, habits,
    haunts, the subject's health;
wanted or not, guilty or not guilty, dead or alive, did
    you see this man

Of course this is hardly to propose that Fearing did not experience a complex, various life, or that his biography would not be engrossing or resonant. Certain episodes particularly circle his poems: his friendships at the University of Wisconsin with the poet Carl Rakosi and with the novelist Margery Latimer, whom he followed to New York in 1924; his writing for the "spicy" pulps, mostly under the pseudonym "Kirk Wolff" ("It Gets to be a Habit" appeared with a Wolff byline in the December 1933 issue of *French Night Life Stories*). Fearing was twice married—to medical social worker Rachel Meltzer and artist Nan Lurie. Each found him remote and secretive. He published film reviews in *New Masses*, briefly toiled for the Chicago City News Bureau, *Time*, and later *Newsweek*, and as a publicist for the Muscular Dystrophy Association of America. He was a regular at Yaddo. When asked by agents of the FBI if he had joined the Communist Party, Fearing famously replied, "Not yet."

This inventive cataloguer of the new American media was himself among the most mediated American poets. During the 1920s and 30s, versions of Fearing appeared as protagonists in at least three novels: the sick, dreamy schoolboy of W. L. River's *Death of a Young Man* (1927), the sardonic idealist of Margery Latimer's *This Is My Body* (1930), and the drunken "ex-poet" turned pulp hack of Albert Halper's *Union Square* (1933). Joseph Mitchell chronicled a further Fearing variant in 1935 for the *New York World Telegraph*: formerly "one of the most fabulous of the city's 'three-bottle men,'" he is now "one of the most respected proletarian poets in the United States." Three years later Anita Tilkin profiled still another Fearing for the *Daily Worker* as a onetime "poet of irony" who recently abandoned "the vein of irony and satire." Beyond a recurrent restlessness, and elusiveness, the portraits all are contradictory. As Fearing wondered at the conclusion of "Radio Blues": "[W]ould you like to tune in upon your very own life, gone somewhere far away." Or as he asked in "A Pattern": "Or are you, in fact, a privileged ghost returned, as usual, to haunt yourself?"

Robert Polito
2003

St. Agnes' Eve

The dramatis personæ include a fly-specked Monday
    evening,
    A cigar store with stagnant windows,
    Two crooked streets,
    Six policemen and Louie Glatz.
Bass drums mumble and mutter an ominous portent
    As Louie Glatz holds up the cigar store and backs out
        with
$14.92.
Officer Dolan noticed something suspicious, it is
        supposed,
    And ordered him to halt,
    But dangerous, handsome, cross-eye'd Louie the rat
Spoke with his gat,
    Rat-a-tat-tat—
    Rat-a-tat-tat
    And Dolan was buried as quickly as possible.
But Louie didn't give a good god damn,
    He ran like a crazy shadow on a shadowy street
    With five policemen off that beat
    Hot on his trail, going Blam! Blam!-blam!
While rat-a-tat-tat
    Rat-a-tat-tat

Said Louie's gat,
So loud that Peter Wendotti rolled away from his wife,
Got out of bed to scratch his stomach and shiver on
the cold floor
Listening to the stammering syllables of instant death
Met on secret floors in the big vacant galleries of
night.
Then Louie sagged and fell and ran.
With seven bullets through his caved-in skull and
those feeble brains
Spilling out like soup.
He crawled behind a water-hydrant and stood them
off for another half minute.
"I'm not shot," he yelled, "I'm not shot," he screamed,
"it isn't me they've shot in the head," he
laughed, "Oh
I don't give a damn!"
And rat-a-tat-tat
Rat-a-tat-tat
Muttered the gat
Of Louie the rat,
While the officers of the law went Blam! Blam!-blam!
Soft music. Violins moan like weeds swaying far under
water.
The vibrant throats of steam-ships hoot a sad
defiance at distance and nothing.
Space curls its arm across the flat roofs and dreary
streets.
Bricks bulge and sag.
Louie's soul arose through his mouth in the form of a
derby hat

That danced with cigarette butts and burned matches
and specks of dust
Where Louie sprawled.
Close-up of Dolan's widow. Of Louie's mother.
Picture of the fly-specked Monday evening and fade
out slow.

Minnie and Mrs. Hoyne

She could die laughing,
On Sunday noon, back of the pawn-shop, under the
smoke-stack, with Mrs. Hoyne.
She could hide her face in rags and die laughing on
the street.
She could snicker in the broom closet. In the dark of
the movies. In bed.
Die, at the way some people talk.
The things they talk about and believe and do.
She and Mrs. Hoyne could sit together and laugh.
Minnie could nicker in the dark alone.
Jesus, what do they mean?
Girls trying to be in love.
People worried about other people. About the world.
Do they own it?
People that don't believe a street is what it looks like.
They think there's more.
There isn't any more, the coo-coos.
She could die laughing.
Free milk for babies, Mrs. Hoyne!

Crazy liars, all of them, and what next?
  Minnie will be a millionaire.
  Mrs. Hoyne will fly a balloon.
  Give my regards to the Queen of France when you
      get there.
  Ask her if she remembers me: "Say, Queen,
  Have you got any old bloomers you don't want, for
      Minnie Spohr?"
  She could die, grinning among the buckets at
      midnight,
  Snicker, staring down the elevator shaft,
  Minnie doesn't care. Get the money!
  She could die laughing some time
  Alone in the broom closet on the forty-third floor.

Andy and Jerry and Joe

(*To Sylvia*)

We were staring at the bottles in the restaurant window,
  We could hear the autos go by,
  We were looking at the women on the boulevard,
  It was cold,
  No one else knew about the things we knew.
We watched the crowd, there was a murder in the
      papers, the wind blew hard, it was dark,
  We didn't know what to do.
  There was no place to go and we had nothing to say,
  We listened to the bells, and voices, and whistles, and
      cars,
  We moved on,

We weren't dull, or wise, or afraid,
We didn't feel tired, or restless, or happy, or sad.
There were a million stars, a million miles, a million
        people, a million words,
A million laughs, a million years,
We knew a lot of things we could hardly understand,
There were liners at sea, and rows of houses, and
        clouds in the sky, and songs in the halls,
We waited on the corner,
The lights were in the stores, there were women on
        the streets, Jerry's father was dead,
We didn't know what we wanted and there was
        nothing to say,
Andy had an auto and Joe had a girl.

Cultural Notes

Professor Burke's symphony "Colorado Vistas"
In four movements,
  I Mountains
  II Canyons
III Dusk
IV Dawn
Was played recently by the Philharmonic.
Snap-shots of the localities described in music were
        passed around.
The audience checked for accuracy.
All O.K.
After the performance Maurice Epstein, twenty-nine,
        tuberculosis,

Stoker on the S.S. Tarboy,

Rose to his feet and shouted:

"He's crazy! Them artists are all crazy,

I can prove it by Max Nordau,

They poison the minds of young girls."

Otto Svoboda, 500 Avenue A, butcher, Pole, husband,
        philosopher,

Argued in rebuttal: "Shut your trap, you!

The question is, does the symphony fit in with Karl
        Marx?"

At the Friday evening meeting of the Browning Writing
        League

Mrs. Whittamore Ralston-Beckett, traveler, lecturer,
        novelist, critic, poet, playwright, editor,
        mother, idealist,

Fascinated her audience in a brief talk, whimsical and
        caustic

Appealing to the younger generation to take a brighter,
        happier, more sunny and less morbid

View of life's unchanging fundamentals.

Mrs. Ralston-Beckett quoted Sir Horace Bennet.

        "O Beauty," she said,

"Take your fingers off my throat, take your elbow out of
        my eye,

Take your sorrow off my sorrow,

Take your hat, take your gloves, take your feet down off
        the table,

Take your beauty off my beauty, and go."

After the performance Maurice Epstein, twenty-nine,
        tuberculosis,

Stoker on the S.S. Tarboy,

Kicked to his feet and screamed:
"She's crazy! Them artists are all crazy!
I can prove it by Max Nordau
They poison the minds of young girls."
Otto Svoboda, butcher, Pole, husband, philosopher,
Spoke in reply: "Shut your trap, you!
The question is, what about Karl Marx?"

John Standish, Artist

(*For J. R. G.*)

If I am to live, or be in the studios,
    If I am to be in the quiet halls and clubs;
    Quiet at tea;
    If I am to talk calmly at dinner, when evening falls,
    If I am to breathe
When it is night, and millions are awake,
    Moving like a sea, not human, not known;
    When millions are aroused to stare, to laugh, to kill;
    When I feel them;
    When they have no voices, but they have mouths and
        eyes;
    When their wants are confused, but implacable;
    When a theory about them becomes nothing, and a
        portrait of them would look well on no studio
        wall;
    When they cringe, when they scream, when they are
        counted by millions;
    When they have no meaning to me, to themselves, to
        the earth; but they are alive;

If I am to live, if I am to breathe,
    I must walk with them a while; laugh with them; stare
        and point;
    Pick one and follow him to the rotted wharves;
Write my name, under his, in grey latrines: "John
        Standish, Artist."
    I must follow him, screaming as he does, through the
        docks, basements, tenements, wharves,
    Follow him till he sleeps, and kill him with a stone.

They Liked It

They watched the lights go on when night fell.
    Away below them streets glowed up
    Like topaz necklaces on black silk.
    They liked the red eye in the Metropolitan.
    And they liked Broadway.
Blake had nothing to do for a while. He talked.
    No one in the office paid attention.
"Listen. I want advice.
    You remember that Swede I was telling about?
    I saw her again last night.
    I'm going crazy."
They liked the muffled hammer and rasp of the city's
        life.
    They liked its size.
    They liked to hear liners in the harbor
    Boom at the sky.
"We went to a flat on Sixty-second.
    There were a lot of her friends along,

And she took on six of them right under my eyes.
But when I barely touched her she laughed in my
    face.
'I'll take any man in the world,' she says, 'but never
    you.'
I've followed her around for two years.
She's driving me crazy.
What should I do?"
Blake wore checkered socks, carried a cane, had a wife
    in the Bronx.
No one knew where he lived.
"Swede!" said one of them.
    "You lying half-wit, the last time you told that story
        the girl was a wop.
    Before that she was Irish.
    Make her a nigger next time."
    Blake laughed.
They liked to feel the city, away below them, stretch out
    and breathe.
    They liked the Metropolitan's red eye, and Broadway.
    They liked to hear liners in the harbor scream at the
        sky.
    They liked it all.

Jack Knuckles Falters But Reads Own Statement at His Execution While Wardens Watch

Has little to say.
Gentlemen, I feel there is little I
    care to say at this moment, but the press has urged me
    to express a few appropriate
Thanks Warden for kindness
    remarks. I
    am grateful to Warden E. J. Springer for the many
    kindnesses he has shown me in the last six weeks and I
    also wish to thank my friends who stuck by me
    to the last. As one who entered
    his nation's defense
Staggers when he sees electric chair
    five days after war was declared I
    was hoping for a pardon from the governor,
    but evidently the government has forgotten its
        veterans
    in a moment of need.
Will Roumania Prince wed again?
    What brought me to the chair
    was keeping bad companions against the advice
    heard three gun-shots and saw a man running
    of my mother and companions. How I wish
Wishes he could have another chance
    I could live my life over again. If I
    could only be given another chance I would show
    the world how to be a man, but I declare
"I am an innocent man," declares Knuckles

before God gentlemen that I am an innocent man,
as innocent as any of you now
heard three gun-shots and saw a man running
standing before me, and the final sworn word I
publish to the world is that Mike Capasuccio
lied his soul to hell. I
Smoke rolls from mouth as current kills
was not on the corner of Lexington and Fifty-ninth
streets
at eight o'clock
heard three gun-shots and saw a man running
and I never saw John Hafmunger in my whole life.

FROM **Aphrodite Metropolis**

II

"Myrtle loves Harry"—It is sometimes
hard to remember a thing like that,
hard to think about it, and no one
knows what to do with it when he has it,
so write it out on a bill-board that stands
under the yellow light of an "L" platform
among popcorn wrappers and cigarette butts,
a placard that says
"Mama I love Crispy Wafers So."
Leave it on a placard where somebody else
gave the blonde lady a pencil moustache,
and another perplexed citizen deposited

"Jesus saves! Jesus saves!"
One can lay this bundle down there with the others
and never lose it, or forget it, or want it.
"Myrtle loves Harry."
They live somewhere.

III

Harry loves Myrtle—He has strong arms
from the warehouse,
and on Sunday when they trolley to emerald meadows
        he doesn't say
"What will your chastity amount to when your flesh
        withers in a little while?"
No,
on Sunday when they trolley to emerald meadows
they look at the Sunday paper
"Girl Slays Banker-Betrayer"
they spread it around on the grass
"Bath-tub Stirs Jersey Row"
and then they sit down on it, nice.
Harry doesn't say "Ziggin's Ointment for withered flesh,
cures thousands of men and women of moles, warts, red
        veins,
flabby throat, scalp and hair diseases,
not expensive, and fully guaranteed."
No, Harry says nothing at all,
he smiles,
and they kiss in the emerald meadows on the Sunday
        paper.

The Drinkers

Except for their clothing and the room,
Gonzetti's basement on MacDougal,
The men are a painting by Franz Hals,
"Flemish Drinkers" or "Burghers of Antwerp."
We have a speakeasy here, however,
Four men drinking gin, three of them drunk.
Outside is the street that sleeps and screams,
Beyond it are other sleeping streets,
And above us, above the paper'd ceiling,
Above Gonzetti's private roof,
Is a black, tremendous sky that crawls.
We have a Village speakeasy here,
One curtained room with ochre lights,
Four men drinking gin, three of them drunk.
Four new men are born in their brains
That would not show in a painting by Hals.
They do not hear each other now—
They listen to voices in themselves
Mad with perfect sanity.
Hals could not show Gonzetti's room
Reeling and stretching out in space.
Hals could not show their brilliant eyes
Watching a thing beyond the walls
Step from air and beckon them
To follow through streets, and nights, and days . . .
We have a speakeasy here, tonight.
Gonzetti for three dollars cash,
Is giving the drinkers ten thousand things
Not Hals or any man could show.

Lithographing

These are the live,
    Not silhouettes or dead men.
    That dull murmur is their tread on the street.
    Those brass quavers are their shouts.
Here is the wind blowing through the crowded square.
    Here is the violence and secret change.
    And these are figures of life beneath the sea.
These are the lovely women
    And the exhilarations that die.
    Here is a stone lying on the side-walk
    In the shadow of the wall.
Hey? What saith the noble poet now,
    Drawing his hand across his brow?
    Claude, is the divine afflatus upon you?
    Hey? Hey Claude?
Here are a million taxi drivers, social prophets,
    The costume for an attitude,
    A back-stage shriek,
    The heat and speed of the earth.
Here is a statue of Burns.
    There is the modern moon.
    That song is the latest dance.
Hey? Of what doth the noble poet brood
    In a tragic mood?

Portrait

William Lowell is drunk again.
> He has escaped the skull-faced men that whisper and
>> wait. Forgotten the filed documents.
> Now there is a reason for his smooth desk, for the
>> rustling papers and white corridors.
> Now there is a reason for his thousand defeats.
> There is a reason for having gone with the whores,
>> lain awake in black rooms, walked through
>> vacant streets, talked to cats in deserted halls,
> If the world knew, there are reasons for having lied
>> and betrayed and cringed.

If the world knew his life,
> Knew the hundred forces seeking to destroy him;
> If there were an eye of god to see him as he is, know
>> his motives in spite of compromise and evasion
>> and fear,
> See him waiting in desolate rooms, cringing at a
>> word, broken by remorse—

William Lowell, born under blue skies,
> Child dreaming under broad pillars of sunlight rising
>> beyond the clouds,
> No fever then, no profane dreams, no skulls following
>> him in roaring tunnels to stare through his
>> eyes into a soul on fire,
> Peace, and no crazy venom in that lost day—

If the world knew,
> There is a reason for his thousand failures, vows,
>> treacheries, lies, escapes,
> And if the world would hear him

William Lowell would be at peace with all mankind
For one hour before the white corridors and vacant
      streets and whispering skulls knew him no
      more,
William Lowell, the child of blue skies.

The Cabinet of Simplicity

It will be known as Doctor Barky's cabinet, a new magic,
      Something for which there can be no substitute.
      May be used as an ornament or worn like a hat.
      Neat. Genteel.
      Doctor Barky's patented magic cabinet of strict, strict
          simplicity.
      Doctor Barky is the type of man who, were he to see a
          photograph of the Himalayas,
      Or of a Zulu headhunter, or of an octopus,
      Would believe that what he saw was, somewhere, real.
      Naïve, credulous as a child, easily excited,
      The doctor's imagination indeed knows no bounds.
      He has looked at an Egyptian mummy and expressed
          faith that it once laughed.
      That problem, however, remains unsolved.
      But the cabinet, the magic box
      In which Doctor Barky has projected the universe
      And reduced life to its simplest terms—
      That is no dream.
      Upside down in a darkened room
      Among an excitable audience, credulous and naïve,

The creaking of the cabinet's hinges could be
  mistaken
For a wordless whispering through space,
For discords struck from violent streets,
For the giant harmonies of death itself.
But a word here about its creator, and what gave life to
  the invention.
Doctor Barky has traveled far.
One time in a dream he cut off his head and gave it to
  a girl with stone lips.
When she drank the acid of his skull,
And later he found her twisted body stretched by the
  sea, burned from within.
The doctor felt sick regret.
But dining on her lips that calm twilight by the frozen
  waves,
Watching the motionless gulls, listening to far-off
  laughter, and musing on the depth of land and
  sky,
He grew content.
When the heat swelled in his bones, he shrieked and
  died.
Centuries later, this time no dream
The doctor as a young boy playing on the beach
Uncovered his smooth skull buried in the sand.
What a meeting!
What undercurrent of pathos was in that gay reunion!
These and other severe but pointless experiences
  Have whetted in Doctor Barky a need to arrange the
  world so that he can understand it,
And still more, to create a fixed world.

See then the cabinet as it will appear before all eyes,
  Swung into space above the stars.
  Magnificent! Magnificent! Magnificent!
  Imagine now the doctor as he doffs his hat,
  Steps forward, bows.
"This is my weapon, the mechanical heart that tames
      chaos.
  In its lower left-hand drawer I have caused to be
      placed
  Spices, gems, perfumes, fruit-rinds, nails,
  Mottos for all family occasions,
  A government investor's guide for the year 1857,
  And half a deck of playing cards said to have been
      used by John Brown
  On the night before he was hanged.
"In the lower right-hand drawer I have placed a set of
      Tennyson,
  And a copy of 'Will the Stars Grow Dim?'—that
      immortal novel by the world-renowned
      author,
  My friend, Mr. B. Phillpston Gibbs.
  I do this thing that the spiritual needs of man be not
      neglected.
"The large upper-chest I have left empty, for the
      public's convenience,
  Save for a small bottle containing my right kidney,
  The result of a most painful operation.
  I thought the public might be interested," said
      Doctor Barky shyly.
  "The kidney is preserved in alcohol."   He chuckled
      whimsically,

There was a twinkle in his eye. "Lucky kidney!"
The doctor has finished.
He steps back into the shadows forever.
Tall candles burn before the magic box.
Inscrutable and still, the mechanical heart draws into
itself
The veins and arteries of chaos.
Earth, time, and space, with a gesture,
Are wound and set again in motion.
Comrade, this is no poem,
Who touches this
Touches Doctor Barky's patented magic cabinet of
certified, strictly guaranteed simplicity and
truth.

Ballad of the Salvation Army

On Fourteenth street the bugles blow,
Bugles blow, bugles blow.
The red, red, red, red banner floats
Where sweating angels split their throats,
Marching in burlap petticoats,
Blow, bugles, blow.

God is a ten car Bronx express,
Red eyes round, red eyes round.
"Oh where is my lustful lamb tonight,
His hair slicked down and his trousers tight?
I'll grind him back to my glory light!"
Roll, subway, roll.

Heaven is a free amusement park,
   Big gold dome, big gold dome.
Movies at night: "The life she led."
Everyone sleeps in one big bed.
The stars go around inside your head.
   Home, sweet home.

On Fourteenth street the bugles blow,
   Bugles blow, bugles blow,
The torpid stones and pavements wake,
A million men and street-cars quake
In time with angel breasts that shake,
   Blow, bugles, blow!

Green Light

Bought at the drug store, very cheap; and later pawned.
   After a while, heard on the street; seen in the park.
   Familiar but not quite recognized.
   Followed and taken home and slept with.
   Traded or sold. Or lost.
Bought again at the corner drug store,
   At the green light, at the patient's demand, at nine
        o'clock.
   Re-read and memorized and re-wound.
   Found unsuitable.
   Smashed, put together, and pawned.
Heard on the street, seen in a dream, heard in the park,
        seen by the light of day,

Carefully observed one night by a secret agent of the
　　　　Greek Hydraulic Mining Commission, in
　　　　plain clothes, off duty.
The agent, in broken English, took copious notes.
　　　　Which he lost.
Strange and yet ordinary.
Sad, but true.
True; or exaggerated; or true;
　　　　As the people laugh and the sparrows fly;
　　　　As the people change and the sea stays;
　　　　As the people go;
　　　　As the lights go on and it is night, and it is serious,
　　　　　　　and it is just the same;
　　　　As some one dies and it is serious and just the same;
　　　　As a girl knows and it is small; and true;
　　　　As a butcher knows and it is true; and pointless;
　　　　As an old man knows and it is comical; and true;
　　　　As the people laugh, as the people think, as the people
　　　　　　　change,
　　　　It is serious and the same; exaggerated; or true.
Bought at the drug store on the corner
　　　　Where the wind blows and the motors go by and it is
　　　　　　　night or day.
　　　　Bought for the hero's pride.
　　　　Bought to instruct the animals in the zoo.
　　　　Bought to impress the statuary in the park.
　　　　Bought for the spirit of the nation's splendid cultural
　　　　　　　heritage.
　　　　Bought to use as a last resort.
　　　　Bought at a cut rate, at a cheap demand, at the green
　　　　　　　light, at nine o'clock.

Borrowed or bought, to look well. To ennoble. To
        prevent disease. To have.
Broken or sold. Or given away.

Breakfast With Hilda

Coffee for Hilda.
Hilda being gay.
Hilda walking in sunlight forever
On streets bright as diamonds.
Hilda dancing.
Hilda dressed in a new green gown.
Coffee for Hilda
While she makes toast.
She is always looking at the sky
As her lover bends down to bruise her mouth
And smooth her hand.
Now, however, in the hushed cathedral
A multitude gathered before the draped bier
Of Hilda, the martyr,
Kneels in reverent prayer.
Hilda in white.
Hilda, sad.
Hilda forgiving the lover who has martyr'd her
And smoothed her hand.
Hilda always kissing him.
Hilda always dancing in an ivory palace
While poets and princes
Are shooting at each other
And stabbing themselves.

She is asleep.
She is awake.
Hilda singing, forever and ever,
While Hilda makes toast,
And Hilda makes coffee,
For Hilda, the gay.

Saturday Night

(For W. L. R.)

That is not blood on the shiny street
    Where heroes and heroines appear
    In taxis bound for bright cabarets.
That is not blood along the pavement, though it could
        be.
    It is dirty water,
    Not the blood you think might be there
    After crowds have scraped and cursed and hammered
        upon it all day.
9:29 Saturday night.
    Elite Max.
    Charlotte, the beautiful magazine girl.
    They want to hear music.
    They only want to hear some music play.
A packed house in Madison Square Garden
    Finds delirium in a prize-fight,
    And elsewhere, others are entertained by Senator
        Horgan's speech.
    But suave Max and lovely Charlotte
    Seek their pleasure at the "Blue Swan."

10:38 P.M.

Battling Bolinska sleeps on the canvas mat.

Senator Horgan is a true statesman of the old school.

Shall we go to the "Parakeet" instead of this place?

It is kind of dull here. Yes.

Give the waiter ten dollars.

That sum represents one day's mental travail

On the part of nonchalant Max, élite haberdasher

Whose cut-priced hosiery shines in a modest window.

But there is no blood on the street

Though crowds have struggled and lied and screamed
upon it all day long.

There is no blood along the pavement from Max,
Charlotte, or anyone

To pay for the hosiery, the "Blue Swan," and the
fatigue.

11:45 Saturday night

On penny arcade and gin palace

And senator alike.

11:45 the great leveller.

That is rain water on the shiny street

Not eyes, not blood, not fingers, nerves, rags, glass,
bones,

Where now in a taxi suave Max and exquisite
Charlotte

Roll onward in each other's arms,

Roll on into the big silhouette of gaiety,

Roll on through Saturday night.

Evening Song

(For H. R.)

Go to sleep McKade.
    Fold up the day. It was a bright scarf.
    Put it away.
    Take yourself apart like a house of cards.
It is time to be a grey mouse under a tall building.
    Go there. Go there now.
    Look at the huge nails. Run behind the pipes.
    Scamper in the walls.
    Crawl toward the beckoning girl, her breasts are
        warm.
    But here is a dead man. A lunatic?
    Kill him with your pistol. Creep past him to the girl.
Sleep, McKade.
    Throw one arm across the bed. Wind your watch.
    You are a gentleman and important.
    Yawn. Go to sleep.
The continent, turning from the sun, is dark and quiet.
    Your ticker waits for tomorrow morning
    And you are alive now.
    It will be a long time before they put McKade under
        the sod.
    Sometime, but not now.
    Sometime, though. Sometime for certain.
Take apart your brain,
    Close the mouths in it that have been hungry, they
        are fed for a while.
    Go to sleep, you are a gentleman McKade, alive and
        sane,

A gentleman of position.
Tip your hat to the lady.
Speak to the mayor.
You are a personal friend of the mayor's, are you not?
True, a friend of the mayor's.
And you met the Queen of Roumania? True.
Then go to sleep.
Be a dog sleeping in the old sun.
Be a dog dreaming in the old sun by the Appian Way.
Be a dog lying in the meadow watching soldiers pass
on the road.
Follow the girl who beckons to you.
Run from the man with the dagger. It will split your
bones.
Be terrified.
Curl up and dream on the pavement of Fifth Avenue
in the old sun.
Sleep, McKade.
Yawn. Go to sleep.

Invitation

We will make love, when the hospitals are quiet and the
blue police car stops to unload prisoners,
We will sleep, while searchlights go across the sky,
We will dine, while the down-and-out actor shakes
hands cordially in an uptown bar,
We will be alone, we will go to the theatre, we will be
drunk, we will die, and there will be a
thousand lovers on the bus-tops, they will find

the suicide lying on the floor in a furnished
room.
It will be morning when the old men are dreaming in
sunlit parks,
It will be night when the movie heroine smiles
through perfect tears,
Night when the cashier is blackmailed and crowds are
muttering in the square, night when a girl
walks with head turned back to watch the
shadows following through dim streets,
It will be night when the judge drinks with the
salesman and the lady novelist bares her soul,
Night when we laugh,
It will be night when pleasure turns to agony, agony
to terror, terror to rage, rage to delight,
It will be morning when we forget,
It will be morning when the air grows warm, and we
read the news.
Here we will be invited by thundering feet, desolate
faces, laughter, cunning eyes, eyes bright with
love, lips tightened in pain,
Here we will be urged by reality confused with
dream,
We will be urged by the hunger of the live, invited by
the relentless purposes of millions,
Here we will be among the living and dead,
With the millions, we will know this and we will
forget,
We will be aroused, we will make love, we will dream,
we will go through endless streets, we will
smile across the room.

Angel Arms

She is the little pink mouse, his far away star,
    The pure angel in his sleep,
    With skirts blowing back over stark, bright thighs,
    And knees that are ivory, or white, or pink,
Pink as the little pink mouse, his far away star,
    The pure angel in a deep dream, his lonely girl.
She is going to be Feldman's girl some day.
    No damn immoral scum will ever kiss her lips,
    No crazy black fiend will ever stain her thighs
    With a touch, or a glance,
    Or dare to think of them,
    Not even Feldman,
    Not anyone, she is so clean,
    She is so pure,
She is so strange, she is so clean,
She is a little pink mouse
    Squeaking among the rubbish and dried tobacco juice
        of black alleys,
    A blazing star among dirty electric lights in
        warehouse lofts,
    A Bible angel smiling up at him from a starched bed,
    Telling him to be a good, pure Feldman . . That's
        what he is . . That's what he is . .
Do they think he is a woman-faced roach,
    A walking sewer, with his girl a bottle-fly buzzing on
        the rim,
    Do they think he is a hunch-backed yellow poodle
    Screaming under the wheels of red engines that
        squawk through streets?

Some day he is going to kill all the morons,
 Be applauded by crowds,
 Praised in the churches,
 Cheered by the gang,
Be smiled upon by the little pink mouse, his far away
   star,
 His pure angel with her skirts torn away over blinding
   thighs,
 She is going to be Feldman's girl some day.
Hand in hand, heart joined to heart,
 A new day dawned,
 Happy and sweet and sunny and pure.
Some hot summer night
 When the city trembles like a forest after battle
 And Feldman's brain is an iron claw
 She will drop from an "L" train sliding through the
   sky like a burning snake
 And give him the wink, and he will come along . .
He will come along . .
She is the little pink mouse that whispers "Coo-coo,
   Feldman!"
 A touch-me-not star,
 His smiling angel with her soft angel arms
 Jerking the barbed wire caught in his bones.

Conclusion

You will give praise to all things, praise without end;
    idly in the morning, bluntly at noon, cunningly with
            the evening cigar, you will meditate further
            praise;
    so will the days pass, each profitable and serene; so
            will your sleep be undisturbed; so you will live;
    no faith will be difficult, rising from doubt; no love
            will be false, born of dread;

In the flaring parks, in the speakeasies, in the hushed
            academies, your murmur will applaud the
            wisdom of a thousand quacks. For theirs is the
            kingdom.
    By your sedate nod in the quiet office you will grieve
            with the magnate as he speaks of sacrifice. For
            his is the power.
    Your knowing glance will affirm the shrewd virtue of
            clown and drudge; directors' room or
            streetcorner, the routine killer will know your
            candid smile; your handclasp, after the
            speeches at the club, will endorse the valor of
            loud suburban heroes. For theirs is the glory
            forever and ever.

Always, more than wise, you will be found with the
          many resolved against the few;
   but you will be a brother, on second thought, to all men.

The metropolitan dive, jammed with your colleagues,
          the derelicts; the skyscraper, owned by your
          twin, the pimp of gumdrops and philanthropy;
          the auditoriums, packed with weeping
          creditors, your peers; the morgues, tenanted
          by your friends, the free dead; the asylums,
          cathedrals, prisons, treasuries, brothels,
          shrines—upon all, all of them you will find
          means to bestow praise,
And as you know, at last, that all of this will be,
   as you walk among millions, indifferent to them,
   or stop and read the journals filled with studied alarm,
   or pause and hear, with no concern, the statesman
          vending manufactured bliss,

You will be grateful for an easy death,
   your silence will praise them for killing you.

Winner Take All

Innocent of the mean or stupid, and innocent of crime,
   still, justice denied you, from this extremity there is
          no escape;
   say to the accusing eyes, say to the doctor standing at
          your deathbed, say to the memory of your
          mistakes, say you are innocent,

Say to the telegram announcing death you are innocent
of death;
say to the ticker that wipes you out this failure was
not to be foreseen,

Tell the black headlines shouting your infamy to
millions that even a judge has to have what he
has to have,
and they say you've been bought, fixed, call it a bribe
when you borrow money from a friend;

Yes, tell the neighbors,
after he's gone, calling you a lowdown doublecrossing
whore,
tell them you are innocent,
a woman's got to have what she's got to have, and you
had to have that man,

Say to the world you are a man of worth, aloof from
days filled with brisk refusal and command,
say you are a gentleman, untouched by the pettiness
forced upon you,
say you, also, are a talking-picture queen, innocent of
vacant nights, useless desires, bargain heroes,

Go on, tell the jury you are innocent of murder,
shooting at an arm reaching for a gun to drop you
dead,
robbery, yes, but you never meant to kill that crazy
fool, yes, robbery,
and who knows how you needed money?—

you've got to have what you've got to have, you're
　　　　going to do what you've got to do,

And you are innocent of what has to happen,
　　　innocent, when they put you out on the street, when
　　　　　　they look at you and laugh, when you grow old
　　　　　　and fade away, when they strap you in the
　　　　　　electric chair,
　　　tell them all you are innocent;

What if they don't listen and there is no escape?
　　　Still you are innocent, and brave, and wise, and strong.

Resurrection

You will remember the kisses, real or imagined;
　　　you will remember the faces that were before you,
　　　　　　and the words exchanged;
　　　you will remember the minute crowded with
　　　　　　meaning, the moment of pain, the aimless
　　　　　　hour;
　　　you will remember the cities, and the plains, and the
　　　　　　mountains, and the sea,

And recall the friendly voice of the killer, or the voice of
　　　　the priest, inhumanly sweet;
　　　recall the triumphant smile of the duped;
　　　you will not forget compassion that glittered in the
　　　　　　eyes of the moneylender, refusing you, nor

forget the purpose that lay beneath the
merchant's warmth;
you will not forget the voice of the bought magistrate
quivering in horror through the courtroom
above prostitute and pimp,
the majesty of the statesman at the microphone, the
sober majesty of the listening clerk,
the face of the fool, radiant on newspaper and screen;

You will remember hope that crawled up the barroom
tap and spoke through the confident speech of
the lost,
happiness clearly displayed on the staring billboards,
love casually revealed in the magazines and novels, or
stated in the trembling limbs of ancient
millionaires,
you will remember the triumph easily defined by the
rebel savior, by the breadloaf in the hand of
the ghetto wife, by the inscription on the
patriot tomb,
you will remember your laughter that rose with the
steam from the carcass on the street
in hatred and pity exactly matched.

These are the things that will return to you,
to mingle vividly with the days and nights, with the
sound of motors and the sun's warmth,
with fatigue and desire,
as you work, and sleep, and talk, and laugh, and die.

Obituary

Take him away, he's as dead as they die.
   Hear that ambulance bell, his eyes are staring straight
      at death.
   Look at the fingers growing stiff, touch the face
      already cold, see the stars in the sky, look at
      the stains on the street,

Look at the ten-ton truck that came rolling along fast
      and stretched him out cold,

Then turn out his pockets and make the crowd move on.
   Sergeant, what was his name? What's the driver's
      name? What's your name, sergeant?
   Go through his clothes,
   take out the cigars, the money, the papers, the keys,
      take everything there is,

And give the dollar and a half to the Standard Oil. It
      was his true-blue friend.
   Give the key of his flat to the D.A.R. They were
      friends of his, the best a man ever had.
   Take out the pawnticket, wrap it, seal it, send it along
      to the People's Gas. They were life-long pals.
      It was more than his brother. They were just
      like twins.

Give away the shoes,
   give his derby away. Donate his socks to the
      Guggenheim fund,

let the Morgans hold the priceless bills, and leaflets,
and racing tips under lock and key,
and give Mr. Hoover the pint of gin.
Because they're all good men. And they were friends
of his.

Don't forget Gene Tunney. Don't forget Will Hays.
Don't forget Al Capone. Don't forget the
I.R.T.
Give them his matches to remember him by.
They lived with him, in the same old world. And
they're good men, too.

That's all, sergeant. There's nothing else, lieutenant.
There's no more, captain.
Pick up the body, feed it, shave it, find it another job.

Have a cigar, driver?
Take two cigars.
You were his true-blue pal.

American Rhapsody (1)

Let us present,
this night of love, and murder, and reckoning, and
sleep,
evening of illusion, night filled with thousands intent
upon ordained ends,
let us introduce, among a few leading citizens in
unrehearsed acts,

That popular ghost, Franklin Devoe, serial hero of the
      current magazines,
    the exact, composite dream of those who read.
    An artist in innocence,
    tonight the ectoplasm of Mr. Devoe hovers
      inescapably everywhere about us,
    that profitable smile invisible above the skyscrapers,
      those serene eyes piercing nightcourts, clinics,
      tenements, that exclusive nicety available in
      remote villages and farms,

That breadline.
    Salvation before coffee and rolls.
    "Last night a number of you gentlemen hurried
      through the banquet and dashed around to the
      mission next door for another slice of bread.
    Is that gratitude? Is that decency? Certified scabies?
      Starvation preferred?"

That genius, that literateur, Theodore True,
    St. Louis boy who made good as an Englishman in
      theory, a deacon in vaudeville, a cipher in
      politics,
    undesirable in large numbers to any community.
    Closing prices: Is This Really a Commercial Age?—
      100. That Anguished Soul of Marcel Proust—
      150. Liberty or Dangerous Freedom, Which?
      —210. That Unknown, Patriotic, Law-abiding
      Corpse—305.

We present that talking-picture queen, and the
    superfilm:
    "Will the daughter of the humble whorehouse
        magnate wed the patrician wardheeler, O
        America?"
    And the Blumberg twins (magistrate Ike, gorilla
        Mike) in conference with that blond, blond
        evangelist.
    The senator at that microphone. Those spinster sibyls
        in the rotogravure. That proprietor of the
        revolution, oracle Steve.

"I killed her because she had an evil eye."   "We are not
        thinking now of our own profits, of course."
        "Nothing can take back from us this night."
        "Let me alone you God damn rat."
        "Two rickeys." "Cash."

These are merely close-ups.
    At a distance these eyes and faces and arms,
    maimed in the expiation of living, scarred in payment
        exacted through knife, hunger, silence, hope,
        exhaustion, regret,
    melt into an ordered design, strange and significant,
        and not without peace.

Dividends

This advantage to be seized; and here, an escape
        prepared against an evil day;
  so it is arranged, consummately, to meet the issues.
        Convenience and order. Necessary murder
        and divorce. A decent repute.

Such are the plans, in clear detail.
  She thought it was too soon but they said no, it was
        too late. They didn't trust the other people.
  Sell now.
  He was a fool to ignore the market. It could be
        explained, he said. With the woman, and after
        the theatre she made a scene. None of them
        felt the crash for a long time.

What is swifter than time?

So it is resolved, upon awakening. This way it is devised,
        preparing for sleep. So it is revealed, uneasily,
        in strange dreams.
  A defense against grey, hungry, envious millions. A
        veiled watch to be kept upon this friend.
  Dread that handclasp. Seek this. Smile.
  They didn't trust the others. They were wary. It
        looked suspicious. They preferred to wait,
        they said.

Gentlemen, here is a statement for the third month,
  and here, Mildred, is the easiest way.

Such is the evidence, convertible to profit. These are
        the dividends, waiting to be used.
Here are the demands again, considered again, and
        again the endless issues are all secure.
Such are the facts. Such are the details. Such are the
        proofs.

Almighty God, these are the plans,
        these are the plans until the last moment of the last
            hour of the last day,
        and then the end. By error or accident.
        Burke of cancer. Jackson out at the secret meeting of
            the board. Hendricks through the window of
            the nineteenth floor.
        Maggots and darkness will attend the alibi.
        Peace on earth. And the finer things.
        So it is all devised.
        Thomas, the car.

X Minus X

Even when your friend, the radio, is still; even when her
            dream, the magazine, is finished; even when
            his life, the ticker, is silent; even when their
            destiny, the boulevard, is bare,
        and after that paradise, the dancehall, is closed; after
            that theatre, the clinic, is dark,

Still there will be your desire, and her desire, and his
            desire, and their desire,

your laughter, their laughter,
your curse and his curse, her reward and their reward,
their dismay and his dismay and her dismay
and yours—
Even when your enemy, the collector, is dead; even
when your counsellor, the salesman, is
sleeping; even when your sweetheart, the
movie queen, has spoken; even when your
friend, the magnate, is gone.

1933

You heard the gentleman, with automatic precision,
speak the truth.
Cheers. Triumph.
And then mechanically it followed the gentleman
lied.
Deafening applause. Flashlights, cameras,
microphones. Floral tribute. Cheers.

Down Mrs. Hogan's alley, your hand with others
reaching among the ashes, cinders, scrapiron,
garbage, you found the rib of sirloin wrapped
in papal documents. Snatched it. Yours by
right, the title clear.
Looked up. Saw lips twitch in the smiling head thrust
from the museum window. "A new deal."

And ran. Escaped. You returned the million dollars. You
        restored the lady's virginity.
You were decorated 46 times in rapid succession by
        the King of Italy. Took a Nobel prize. Evicted
        again, you went downtown, slept at the
        movies, stood in the breadline, voted yourself
        a limousine.
Rage seized the Jewish Veterans of Foreign Wars. In
        footnotes, capitals, Latin, italics, the poet of
        the Sunday supplements voiced steamheated
        grief. The RFC expressed surprise.
And the news, at the Fuller Brush hour, leaked out.
Shouts. Cheers. Stamping of feet. Blizzard of confetti.
        Thunderous applause.

But the stocks were stolen. The pearls of the actress,
        stolen again. The bonds embezzled.
Inexorably, the thief pursued. Captured inexorably.
        Tried. Inexorably acquitted.
And again you heard the gentleman, with automatic
        precision, speak the truth.
Saw, once more, the lady's virginity restored.

In the sewers of Berlin, the directors prepared, the room
        dark for the seance, she a simple Baroness, you
        a lowly millionaire, came face to face with
        John D. Christ.
Shook hands, his knife at your back, your knife at his.
        Sat down.
Saw issue from his throat the ectoplasm of Pius VIII,
        and heard "A test of the people's faith." You

said amen, voted to endorse but warned
against default, you observed the astral form of
Nicholas II, and heard "Sacred union of all."
Saw little "Safe for democracy" Nell. Listened
to Adolph "Safety of France and society"
Thiers.
And beheld the faith, the union of rags, blackened
hands, stacked carrion, breached barricades in
flame,
no default, credit restored, Union Carbide 94 3/8, call
money 10%, disarm, steel five points up, rails
rise, Dupont up, disarm, disarm, and heard
again,
ghost out of ghost out of ghost out of ghost,
the voice of the senator reverberate through all the
morgues of all the world, echo again for
liberty in the catacombs of Rome, again sound
through the sweatshops, ghettoes, factories,
mines, hunger again repealed, circle the
London cenotaph once more annulling death,
saw ten million dead returned to life, shot
down again, again restored,

Heard once more the gentleman speak, with automatic
precision, the final truth,
once more beheld the lady's virginity, the lady's
decency, the lady's purity, the lady's innocence,
paid for, certified, and restored.

Crawled amorously into bed. Felt among the maggots
for the mouldering lips. The crumbled arms.
Found them.

Tumult of cheers. Music and prayer by the YMCA.
Horns, rockets. Spotlight.
The child was nursed on government bonds. Cut its
teeth on a hand grenade. Grew fat on
shrapnel. Bullets. Barbed wire. Chlorine gas.
Laughed at the bayonet through its heart.
These are the things you saw and heard, these are the
things you did, this is your record,
you.

Dear Beatrice Fairfax:

*Is it true that Father Coughlin and Miss Aimee
Semple McPherson and General Hugh Johnson and
Mrs. Barbara Mdivani and Mr. Samuel Insull and
Miss Greta Garbo and Mr. Prince Mike Romanoff?*

Foolproof baby with that memorized smile,
burglarproof baby, fireproof baby with that rehearsed
appeal,
reconditioned, standardized, synchronized, amplified,
best-by-test baby with those push-the-button
tears,

Your bigtime sweetheart worships you and you alone,
your goodtime friend lives for you, only you,
he loves you, trusts you, needs you, respects you,
gives for you, fascinated, mad about you,
all wrapped up in you like the accountant in the trust,
like the banker trusts the judge, like the judge

respects protection, like the gunman needs his
needle, like the trust must give and give—

He's with you all the way from the top of the bottle to
the final alibi,
from the handshake to the hearse, from the hearse to
the casket,
to the handles on the casket, to the nails, to the
hinges, to the satin, to the flowers, to the
music, to the prayer, to the graveyard, to the
tomb,

But just the same, baby, and never forget,
it takes a neat, smart, fast, good, sweet doublecross
to doublecross the gentleman who doublecrossed the
gentleman who doublecrossed
your doublecrossing, doublecrossing, doublecross
friend.

American Rhapsody (2)

She said did you get it, and he said did you get it,
at the clinic, at the pawnshop, on the breadline, in
jail,
shoes and a roof and the rent and a cigarette and
bread and a shirt and coffee and sleep—

Reaching at night for a bucket of coal among the B & O
flats in the B & O yards,

they said there's another one, get him they said,
or staring again at locked and guarded factory gates;
or crouched in a burglarproof loft, hand
around a gun; or polite, urgent, face before a
face behind a steelbarred cage:

All winter she came there, begging for milk. So we had
the shacks along the river destroyed by police.
But at the uptown exhibit a rich, vital
sympathy infused the classic mood. When
muriatic acid in the whiskey failed, and
running him down with an auto failed, and
ground glass failed, we finished the job by
shoving a gastube down his throat.
Next year, however, we might have something
definite,

Mountains or plains, crossroads, suburbs, cities or the
sea,
did you take it, was it safe, did you buy it, did you beg
it, did you steal it, was it known,

Name, address, relatives, religion, income, sex, bank
account, insurance, health, race, experience,
age,
out beyond the lunatic asylum, on the city dump; on
the junkheap past the bank, past the church,
past the jungle, past the morgue,
where rats eat the crusts and worms eat the satins and
maggots eat the mould
and fire eats the headlines, eats the statements and the
pictures, eats the promises and proofs, eats the

rind of an orange and a rib and a claw and a
skull and an eye,

Did you find it, was it there, did they see you, were they
waiting, did they shoot, did they stab, did they
burn, did they kill—
one on the gallows and one on the picketline and one
in the river and one on the ward and another
one slugged and another one starved and
another insane and another by the torch.

As the Fuse Burns Down

What will you do, when the phone rings, and they say
to you: What will you do?
What will you say, when the sun lights all the avenue
again, and the battle monument still reads:
These dead did not die in vain?
When night returns, when the clock strikes one, the
clock strikes two, three, four, when the city
sleeps, awakes, when day returns, what will
you say, feel, believe, do,

Do with the culture found in a tabloid, what can be
done with a Lydia Pinkham ad?
What reply can you give to the pawnclerk's decent bid
for your silverware?
How are you to be grateful as "Thrift" glares out
across the ghetto night; reassured, as the
legless, sightless one extends his cup; who can

be surprised, why, how, as the statesman speaks
for peace and moves for war?
Then, when they tell you the executioner does the
best that he can, what can you say? What
then?

Or they come to you, as human fingers comb the city's
refuse, and say, look, you have been saved;
when they tell you, see, you were right, and it is the
day the utilities evidence has been destroyed;
as the state is saved again, three dead, six shot, and
they tell you, look, you have survived, the
reward is yours, you have won—what then?
What then?

What will you say and where will you turn?
What will you do? What will you do? What will you
do?

No Credit

Whether dinner was pleasant, with the windows lit by
gunfire, and no one disagreed; or whether,
later, we argued in the park, and there was a
touch of vomit-gas in the evening air;
Whether we found a greater, deeper, more perfect
love, by courtesy of Camels, over NBC;
whether the comics amused us, or the
newspapers carried a hunger death, and

published a whitehouse prayer for mother's
day;
whether the bills were paid or not, whether or not we
had our doubts, whether we spoke our minds
at Joe's, and the receipt said "Not
Redeemable," and the cash register rang up
"No Sale,"
whether the truth was then, or later, or whether the
best had already gone—

Nevertheless, we know; as every turn is measured; as
every unavoidable risk is known;
as nevertheless, the flesh grows old, dies, dies in its
only life, is gone;
the reflection goes from the mirror; as the shadow, of
even a Communist, is gone from the wall;
as nevertheless, the current is thrown and the wheels
revolve; and nevertheless, as the word is
spoken and the wheat grows tall and the ships
sail on—

None but the fool is paid in full; none but the broker,
none but the scab is certain of profit;
the sheriff alone may attend a third degree in formal
attire; alone, the academy artists multiply in
dignity as a trooper's bayonet guards the door;
only Steve, the side-show robot, knows content; only
Steve, the mechanical man in love with a
photo-electric beam, remains aloof; only
Steve, who sits and smokes or stands in salute,
is secure;

Steve, whose shoebutton eyes are blind to terror,
       whose painted ears are deaf to appeal, whose
       welded breast will never be slashed by bullets,
       whose armature soul can hold no fear.

Dirge

1-2-3 was the number he played but today the number
       came 3-2-1;
   bought his Carbide at 30 and it went to 29; had the
       favorite at Bowie but the track was slow—

O, executive type, would you like to drive a floating
       power, knee-action, silk-upholstered six? Wed
       a Hollywood star? Shoot the course in 58?
       Draw to the ace, king, jack?
   O, fellow with a will who won't take no, watch out for
       three cigarettes on the same, single match; O,
       democratic voter born in August under Mars,
       beware of liquidated rails—

Denouement to denouement, he took a personal pride
       in the certain, certain way he lived his own,
       private life,
   but nevertheless, they shut off his gas; nevertheless,
       the bank foreclosed; nevertheless, the landlord
       called; nevertheless, the radio broke,

And twelve o'clock arrived just once too often,
    just the same he wore one grey tweed suit, bought
            one straw hat, drank one straight Scotch,
            walked one short step, took one long look,
            drew one deep breath,
    just one too many,

And wow he died as wow he lived,
    going whop to the office and blooie home to sleep
            and biff got married and bam had children and
            oof got fired,
    zowie did he live and zowie did he die,

With who the hell are you at the corner of his casket,
            and where the hell we going on the right-hand
            silver knob, and who the hell cares walking
            second from the end with an American Beauty
            wreath from why the hell not,

Very much missed by the circulation staff of the New
            York Evening Post; deeply, deeply mourned by
            the B.M.T.,

Wham, Mr. Roosevelt; pow, Sears Roebuck; awk, big
            dipper; bop, summer rain;
    Bong, Mr., bong, Mr., bong, Mr., bong.

What If Mr. Jesse James Should Some Day Die?

Where will we ever again find food to eat, clothes to
       wear, a roof and a bed, now that the Wall
       street plunger has gone to his hushed,
       exclusive, paid-up tomb?
  How can we get downtown today, with the traction
       king stretched flat on his back in the sand at
       Miami Beach?
  And now that the mayor has denounced the bankers,
       now that the D. A. denies all charges of graft,
       now that the clergy have spoken in defense of
       the home,

O, dauntless khaki soldier, O, steadfast pauper,
       O, experienced vagrant, O, picturesque
       mechanic, O, happy hired man,
  O, still unopened skeleton, O, tall and handsome
       target, O, neat, thrifty, strong, ambitious,
       brave prospective ghost,

Is there anything left for the people to do, is there
       anything at all that remains unsaid?

But who shot down the man in the blue overalls? Who
       stopped the milk? Who took the mattress, the
       table, the birdcage, and piled them in the
       street? Who drove teargas in the picket's face?
       Who burned the crops? Who killed the herd?
       Who leveled the walls of the packingbox city?
       Who held the torch to the Negro pyre? Who

stuffed the windows and turned on the gas for
the family of three?

No more breadlines. No more blackjacks. No more
Roosevelts. No more Hearsts.

No more vag tanks, Winchells, True Stories, deputy
sheriffs, no more scabs.

No more trueblue, patriotic, doublecross leagues. No
more Ku Klux Klan. No more heart-to-heart
shakedowns. No more D.A.R.

No more gentlemen of the old guard commissioned to
safeguard, as chief commanding blackguard in
the rearguard of the home guard, the 1 inch,
3 inch, 6 inch, 10 inch, 12 inch.
no more 14, 16, 18 inch shells.

Escape

Acid for the whorls of the fingertips; for the face, a
surgeon's knife; oblivion to the name;
eyes, hands, color of hair, condition of teeth, habits,
haunts, the subject's health;
wanted or not, guilty or not guilty, dead or alive, did
you see this man

Walk in a certain distinctive way through the public
streets or the best hotels,

turn and go,
escape from marshals, sheriffs, collectors, thugs; from
       the landlord's voice or a shake of the head;
       leave an afternoon beer; go from an evening
       cigar in a wellknown scene,
walk, run, slip from the earth into less than air?

Gone from the teletype, five-feet ten; lost from the
       headlines, middle-aged, grey, posed as a
       gentleman;
a drawling voice in a blue serge suit, fled from the
       radio, forehead scarred,

Tear up the letters and bury the clothes, throw away the
       keys, file the number from the gun, burn the
       record of birth, smash the name from the
       tomb, bathe the fingers in acid, wrap the bones
       in lime,
forget the street, the house, the name, the day,

But something must be saved from the rise and fall of
       the copper's club; something must be kept
       from the auctioneer's hammer; something
       must be guarded from the rats and the fire on
       the city dump;
something, for warmth through the long night of
       death; something to be saved from the last
       parade through granite halls and go, go free,
       arise with the voice that pleads not guilty,
go with the verdict that ascends forever beyond steel-
       barred windows into blue, deep space,

Guilty of vagrancy, larceny, sedition, assault,
    tried, convicted, sentenced, paroled, imprisoned,
        released, hunted, seized,
    under what name and last seen where? And in what
        disguise did the soiled, fingerprinted, bruised,
        secondhand, worndown, scarred, familiar
        disguise escape?

No name, any name, nowhere, nothing, no one, none.

$2.50

But that dashing, dauntless, delphic, diehard, diabolic
        cracker likes his fiction turned with a certain
        elegance and wit; and that anti-anti-anti slum-
        congestion clublady prefers romance;
    search through the mothballs, comb the lavender and
        lace,
    were her desires and struggles futile or did an innate
        fineness bring him at last to a prouder, richer
        peace in a world gone somehow mad?

We want one more compelling novel, Mr. Filbert
        Sopkins Jones,
    all about it, all about it,
    with signed testimonials to its stark, human, while-u-
        wait, iced-or-heated, taste-that-sunshine
        tenderness and truth;

one more comedy of manners, Sir Warwick Aldous
      Wells, involving three blond souls; tried in the
      crucible of war, Countess Olga out-of-limbo
      by Hearst through the steerage peerage,
glamorous, gripping, moving, try it, send for a 5 cent,
      10 cent sample, restores faith to the flophouse,
      workhouse, warehouse, whorehouse, bughouse
      life of man,
just one more long poem that sings a more heroic
      age, baby Edwin, 58,

But the faith is all gone,
      and all the courage is gone, used up, devoured on the
      first morning of a home relief menu,
      you'll have to borrow it from the picket killed last
      Tuesday on the fancy knitgoods line;
      and the glamor, the ice for the cocktails, the shy
      appeal, the favors for the subdeb ball? O.K.,
O.K.,
      but they smell of exports to the cannibals,
      reek of something blown away from the muzzle of a
      twenty inch gun;

Lady, the demand is for a dream that lives and grows
      and does not fade when the midnight theater
      special pulls out on track 15;
      cracker, the demand is for a dream that stands and
      quickens and does not crumble when a
      General Motors dividend is passed;

lady, the demand is for a dream that lives and grows
     and does not die when the national guardsmen
     fix those cold, bright bayonets;
cracker, the demand is for a dream that stays, grows
     real, withstands the benign, afternoon vision
     of the clublady, survives the cracker's evening
     fantasy of honor, and profit, and grace.

American Rhapsody (3)

Before warmth and sight and sound are gone,
     and sometime the evening lights spring up, as always,
          but not for you and not for me,
     before the sky is lost, before the clouds are lost,
          before their slow, still shadows are lost from
          the hills,

Shall we meet at 8 o'clock and kiss and exclaim and
          arrange another meeting as though there were
          love,
     pretend, even alone, we believe the things we say,
     laugh along the boulevard as though there could be
          laughter,
     make our plans and nourish hope, pretending, what is
          the truth, that we ourselves are fooled?

You can be a princess and I'll be the beggar; no, you can
          be the beggar, and I'll be the king;
     you be the mother and go out and beg for food; I'll be
          a merchant, the man you approach, a devoted

husband, famous as a host; the merchant can
be a jobless clerk who sleeps on subway
platforms then lies dead in Potter's field; the
clerk can be a priest, human, kindly, one who
enjoys a joke; the priest can be a lady in jail for
prostitution and the lady can be a banker who
has his troubles, too;
let the merchant be grieved, let the priest be stirred,
let the banker be moved, let the red squad
copper be a patron of the arts;
you be a rat; I'll be the trap; or we both can be
maggots in the long black box;
murder can be comic and hunger can be kind.

Lullaby

Wide as this night, old as this night is old and young as
it is young, still as this, strange as this,
filled as this night is filled with the light of a moon as
grey;
dark as these trees, heavy as this scented air from the
fields, warm as this hand,
as warm, as strong,

Is the night that wraps all the huts of the south and folds
the empty barns of the west;
is the wind that fans the roadside fire;
are the trees that line the country estates, tall as the
lynch trees, as straight, as black;

is the moon that lights the mining towns, dim as the
      light upon tenement roofs, grey upon the
      hands at the bars of Moabit, cold as the bars of
      the Tombs.

20th Century Blues

What do you call it, bobsled champion, and you, too,
      Olympic roller-coaster ace,
   high-diving queen, what is the word,
   number one man on the Saturday poker squad,
      motion picture star incognito as a home girl,
      life of the party or you, the serious type, what
      is it, what is it,

When it's just like a fever shooting up and up and up
      but there are no chills and there is no fever,
   just exactly like a song, like a knockout, like a dream,
      like a book,

What is the word, when you know that all the lights of
      all the cities of all the world are burning bright
      as day, and you know that some time they all
      go out for you,
   or your taxi rolls and rolls through streets made of
      velvet, what is the feeling, what is the feeling,
      when the radio never ends, but the hour, the
      swift, the electric, the invisible hour does not
      stop and does not turn,

what does it mean, when the get-away money burns
in dollars big as moons, but where is there to
go that's just exactly right,
what have you won, plunger, when the 20 to 1 comes
in, what have you won, salesman, when the
dotted line is signed, True Confession lover,
when her eyelids flutter shut at last, what have
you really, really won,
and what is gone, soldier, soldier, step-and-a-half
marine who saw the whole world, hot-tip
addict, what is always just missed, picker of
crumbs, how much has been lost, denied, what
are all the things destroyed,

Question mark, question mark, question mark, question
mark,
and you, fantasy Frank, and dreamworld Dora, and
hallucination Harold, and delusion Dick, and
nightmare Ned,

What is it, how do you say it, what does it mean, what's
the word,
that miracle thing, the thing that can't be so, quote,
unquote, but just the same it's true,
that third-rail, million-volt exclamation mark, that
ditto, ditto, ditto,
that stop, stop, go.

Denouement

Sky, be blue, and more than blue; wind, be flesh and
        blood; flesh and blood, be deathless;
  walls, streets, be home;
  desire of millions, become more real than warmth
        and breath and strength and bread;
  clock, point to the decisive hour and, hour without
        name when stacked and waiting murder fades,
        dissolves, stay forever as the world grows new;

Truth, be known, be kept forever, let the letters, letters,
        souvenirs, documents, snapshots, bills be
        found at last, be torn away from a world of
        lies, be kept as final evidence, transformed
        forever into more than truth;
  change, change, rows and rows and rows of figures,
        spindles, furrows, desks, change into paid-up
        rent and let the paid-up rent become South
        Sea music;
  magic film, unwind, unroll, unfold in silver on that
        million mile screen, take us all, bear us again
        to the perfect denouement,

Where everything lost, needed, each forgotten thing, all
        that never happens,
  gathers at last into a dynamite triumph, a rainbow
        peace, a thunderbolt kiss,
  for you, the invincible, and I, grown older, and he, the
        shipping clerk, and she, an underweight blond
        journeying home in the last express.

2

But here is the body found lying face down in a burlap
              sack, strangled in the noose jerked shut by
              these trussed and twisted and frantic arms;
      but here are the agents come to seize the bed;
      but here is the vase holding saved-up cigarstore
              coupons, and here is a way to save on cigars
              and to go without meat;
      but here is the voice that strikes around the world,
              "My friends . . . my friends," issues from the
              radio and thunders "My friends" in newsreel
              close-ups, explodes across headlines, "Both
              rich and poor, my friends, must sacrifice,"
              re-echoes, murmuring, through hospitals,
              deathcells, "My friends . . . my friends . . .
              my friends . . . my friends . . ."

And who, my friend, are you?
      Are you the one who leaped to the blinds of the
              cannonball express? Or are you the one who
              started life again with three dependents and a
              pack of cigarettes?

But how can these things be made finally clear in a post-
              mortem room with the lips taped shut and the
              blue eyes cold, wide, still, blind, fixed beyond
              the steady glare of electric lights, through the
              white-washed ceiling and the crossmounted
              roof, past the drifting clouds?

Objection, over-ruled, exception, proceed:

Was yours the voice heard singing one night in a
                  flyblown, sootbeamed, lost and forgotten
                  Santa Fe saloon? Later bellowing in rage? And
                  you boiled up a shirt in a Newark furnished
                  room? Then you found another job, and
                  pledged not to organize or go on strike?

We offer this union book in evidence. We offer these
                  rent receipts in evidence. We offer in evidence
                  this vacation card marked, "This is the life.
                  Regards to all."

You, lodge member, protestant, crossborn male, the
                  placenta discolored, at birth, by syphilis, you,
                  embryo four inches deep in the seventh
                  month,
         among so many, many sparks struck and darkened at
                  conception,
         which were you,
         you, six feet tall on the day of death?

Then you were at no time the senator's son? Then you
                  were never the beef king's daughter, married in
                  a storm of perfume and music and laughter
                  and rice?
         And you are not now the clubman who waves and
                  nods and vanishes to Rio in a special plane?
         But these are your lungs, scarred and consumed?
                  These are your bones, still marked by rickets?
                  These are your pliers? These are your fingers,
                  O master mechanic, and these are your cold,
                  wide, still, blind eyes?

The witness is lying, lying, an enemy, my friends, of
Union Gas and the home:

But how will you know us, wheeled from the icebox and
stretched upon the table with the belly slit
wide and the entrails removed, voiceless as the
clippers bite through ligaments and flesh and
nerves and bones,
but how will you know us, attentive, strained, before
the director's desk, or crowded in line in front
of factory gates,
but how will you know us through ringed
machinegun sights as we run and fall in
gasmask, steel helmet, flame-tunic, uniform,
bayonet, pack,
but how will you know us, crumbled into ashes, lost
in air and water and fire and stone,
how will you know us, now or any time, who will ever
know that we have lived or died?

And this is the truth? So help you God, this is the truth?
The truth in full, so help you God? So help
you God?
But the pride that was made of iron and could not be
broken, what has become of it, what has
become of the faith that nothing could destroy,
what has become of the deathless hope,
you, whose ways were yours alone, you, the one like
no one else, what have you done with the hour

you swore to remember, where is the hour, the
day, the achievement that would never die?

Morphine. Veronal. Veronal. Morphine. Morphine.
Morphine. Morphine.

3

Leaflets, scraps, dust, match-stubs strew the linoleum
that leads upstairs to the union hall, the walls
of the basement workers' club are dim and
cracked and above the speaker's stand
Vanzetti's face shows green, behind closed
doors the committeeroom is a fog of smoke,

Who are these people?

All day the committee fought like cats and dogs and
twelve of Mr. Kelly's strongarm men patrolled
the aisles that night, them blackjack guys get
ten to twenty bucks a throw, the funds were
looted, sent to Chicago, at the meeting the
section comrade talked like a fool, more scabs
came through in trucks guarded by police,
workers of the world, workers of the world, workers
of the world,

Who are these people and what do they want, can't they
be decent, can't they at least be calm and
polite,
besides the time is not yet ripe, it might take years,
like Mr. Kelly said, years,

Decades black with famine and red with war, centuries
        on fire, ripped wide,

Who are these people and what do they want, why do
        they walk back and forth with signs that say
        "Bread Not Bullets," what do they mean
        "They Shall Not Die" as they sink in clouds of
        poison gas and fall beneath clubs, hooves,
        rifles, fall and do not arise, arise, unite,
    never again these faces, arms, eyes, lips,

Not unless we live, and live again,
    return, everywhere alive in the issue that returns,
        clear as light that still descends from a star
        long cold, again alive and everywhere visible
        through and through the scene that comes
        again, as light on moving water breaks and
        returns, heard only in the words, as millions of
        voices become one voice, seen only in millions
        of hands that move as one,

Look at them gathered, raised, look at their faces,
        clothes, who are these people, who are these
        people,
    what hand scrawled large in the empty prison cell "I
        have just received my sentence of death. Red
        Front," whose voice screamed out in the
        silence "Arise"?

And all along the waterfront, there, where rats gnaw
        into the loading platforms, here, where the

wind whips at warehouse corners, look, there,
here,
everywhere huge across the walls and gates "Your
party lives,"
where there is no life, no breath, no sound, no touch,
no warmth, no light but the lamp that shines
on a trooper's drawn and ready bayonet.

En Route

No violence
 feeling may run high for a time but remember, no
    violence
 and hurry, this moment of ours may not return

But we will meet again? Yes, yes, now go
 take only the latest instruments, use trained men in
    conservative tweeds who know how to keep
    their mouths shut
 the key positions must be held at all costs
 bring guns, ropes, kerosene, it may be hard to
    persuade our beloved leader there must be no
    violence, no violence

No violence, nothing left to chance, no hysteria, and
    above all no sentiment
 the least delay, the slightest mistake, means the end,
    yes, the end
 why, are you worried?

What is there to be worried about? It's fixed, I tell you,
    fixed, there's nothing to it, listen

we will meet across the continents and years at 4 A.M.
      outside the Greek's when next the barometer
      reads 28.28 and the wind is from the South
      South-East bringing rain and hail and fog and
      snow
until then I travel by dead reckoning and you will take
      your bearings from the stars

I cannot tell you more except this, when you give the
      sign our agent will approach and say: Have
      you seen the handwriting? Then your man is
      to reply: We have brought the money
so we will make ourselves known to each other
and it will be the same as before, perhaps even better,
      and we will arrange to meet again, as always,
      and say goodbye as now, and as we always will,
      and it will be O.K., now go

But what if the police find out? What if the wires are
      down? What if credit is refused? What if the
      banks fail? What if war breaks out? What if
      one of us should die?
What good can all this be to you, or to us, or to
      anyone? Think of the price

What are you trying to do, be funny? This is serious
      hurry
      we must be prepared for anything, anything,
            anything.

Happy New Year

Speak as you used to
    make the drinks and talk while you mix them, as you
        have so many times before

IF IT IS TRUE THAT THE WORLD IS FOR SALE

Then say it, say it once and forget it, drop it, tell how it
            was at bridge or the grocer's
    repeat what you said, what the grocer said, what the
            errand boy said, what the janitor said
    say anything at all

BUT IF IT IS TRUE THAT THE NERVE AND BREATH AND
    PULSE ARE FOR SALE

Tell how it was in some gayer city or brighter place,
            speak of some bloodier, hungrier, more
            treacherous time
    any other age, any far land

BUT IF IT IS TRUE

Forget the answers that give no reason, forget the
            reasons that do not explain
    do you remember the day at the lake, the evening at
            Sam's, the petrified forest, would you like to
            see Paris in June once more

BUT IF IT IS TRUE, IF IT IS TRUE THAT ONLY LIARS LOVE
        TRUTH

Pour the cocktails
    it is late, it is cold, it is still, it is dark
    quickly, for time is swift and it is late, late, later than
        you think
    with one more hour, one more night, one more day
        somehow to be killed.

Literary

I sing of simple people and the hardier virtues, by
            Associated Stuffed Shirts & Company,
            Incorporated, 358 West 42d Street, New York,
            brochure enclosed
    of Christ on the Cross, by a visitor to Calvary, first
            class
    art deals with eternal, not current verities, revised
            from last week's Sunday supplement
    guess what we mean, in *The Literary System*, and a
            thousand noble answers to a thousand empty
            questions, by a patriot who needs the dough.

And so it goes.
    Books are the key to magic portals. Knowledge is
            power. Give the people light.
    Writing must be such a nice profession.
    Fill in the coupon. How do you know? Maybe you
            can be a writer, too.

Lunch With the Sole Survivor

Meaning what it seems to when the day's receipts are
        counted and locked inside the store and the
        keys are taken home
    feeling as it does to drive a car that rides and rides like
        a long, low, dark, silent streak of radio waves
    just the way the hero feels in a smash-hit show
    exactly like the giant in a Times Square sign making
        love across the sky to a lady made of light

And then as though the switch were thrown and all of
        the lights went out
    then as though the curtain fell and then they swept
        the aisles and then it's someone's turn to go
    smoke the last cigarette, drink the last tall drink, go
        with the last long whistle of the midnight train
        as it fades among the hills

Meaning what it seems to mean but feeling the way it
        does
    as though the wind would always, always blow away
        from home.

Devil's Dream

But it never could be
    how could it ever happen if it never did before and it's
        not so now

But suppose that the face behind those steel prison bars
      why do you dream about a face lying cold in the
            trenches streaked with rain and dirt and blood
      is it the very same face seen so often in the mirror
      just as though it could be true

But what if it is, what if it is, what if it is, what if the
            thing that cannot happen really happens just
            the same
      suppose the fever goes a hundred, then a hundred and
            one
      what if Holy Savings Trust goes from 98 to 88 to 78
            to 68, then drops down to 28 and 8 and out of
            sight
      and the fever shoots a hundred two, a hundred three,
            a hundred four, then a hundred five and out

But now there's only the wind and the sky and sunlight
            and the clouds
      with everyday people walking and talking as they
            always have before along the everyday street
      doing ordinary things with ordinary faces and
            ordinary voices in the ordinary way
      just as they always will

Then why does it feel like a bomb, why does it feel like
            a target
      like standing on the gallows with the trap about to
            drop
      why does it feel like a thunderbolt the second before
            it strikes, why does it feel like a tightrope walk
            high over hell

Because it is not, will not, never could be true
    that the whole wide, bright, green, warm, calm world
        goes
CRASH.

Hold the Wire

If the doorbell rings and we think we were followed
        here, if the bell should ring but we are not sure
    how can we decide

IF IT'S ONLY THE GASMAN it may be all right, IF HE'S AN
        AUTHORIZED PERSON IN A DOUBLE-BREASTED
        SUIT we'd better get it over with, but IF HE'S
        SOME NOBODY it may be good news
    or it might mean death IF THE SAMPLES ARE FREE

HOW DO WE KNOW YOU'RE THE PERSON THAT YOU SAY

Decide, decide
    we'd better be certain if we live just once, and the
        sooner the better if we must decide

BUT NOT IF IT'S WAR
    not until we've counted the squares on the wallpaper
        over and added up the circles and the circles
        match the squares
    shall we move to the Ritz if rails go up, or live in
        Potter's Field if the market goes down

if they sign for peace we return to the city, if they
        burn and bomb the city we will go to the
        mountains
who will kill us, if they do, and who will carry on our
        work

Who are you, who are you, you have the right number
        but the connection's very poor
we can hear you well enough but we don't like what
        you're saying
yes, the order was received, but we asked for
        something else

Are you the inventor who wants to sell us an invisible
        man
WE'D LIKE TO BUY HIM BUT WE HAVEN'T GOT THE
        PRICE
are you someone very famous from the Missing
        Persons Bureau but you can't recall the name
COME AROUND NEXT AUGUST, WE'RE BUSY AS HELL
        TODAY
if it's another bill collector there is no one here at all

If it's Adolf Hitler, if it's the subway gorilla, if it's Jack
        the Ripper
SEND HIM IN, SEND HIM IN, IF IT'S JOLLY JACK THE
        RIPPER IN A DOUBLE-BREASTED SUIT AND
        THE SAMPLES ARE FREE.

Longshot Blues

What if all the money is bet on the odd
    maybe the even wins
    what if odd wins but it wins too late

Whoever, wherever
    ever knows who will be just the very one
    this identical day at just this very, very, very, very hour

Whose whole life falls between roto-press wheels
        moving quicker than light, to reappear,
        gorgeous and calm, on page eighteen
    who reads all about it: Prize-winning beauty trapped,
        accused

Who rides, and rides, and rides the big bright limited
        south, or is found, instead, on the bedroom
        floor with a stranger's bullet through the
        middle of his heart
    clutching at a railroad table of trains to the south
        while the curtains blow wild and the radio
        plays and the sun shines on, and on, and on,
        and on
    never having dreamed, at 9 o'clock, it would ever, at
        10 o'clock, end this way

Forever feeling certain, but never quite guessing just
        exactly right
    as no man, anywhere, ever, ever, ever, ever, ever
        knows for sure

Who wins the limousine, who wins the shaving cup,
        who nearly wins the million dollar sweeps
    who sails, and sails, and sails the seven seas
    who returns safe from the fight at the millgates, or
            wins, and wins, and wins, and wins the plain
            pine coffin and a union cortege to a joblot
            grave

With that long black midnight hour at last exploding
        into rockets of gold
    with every single cloud in the sky forever white and
            every white cloud always the winner in its race
            with death
    with every pair of eyes burning brighter than the
            diamonds that burn on every throat
    with every single inch of the morning all yours and
            every single inch of the evening yours alone,
            and all of always, always, altogether new.

A Pattern

The alarm that shatters sleep, at least, is real
    certainly the razor is real, and there is no denying the
    need for coffee and an egg
        are there any questions, or is this quite clear, and
        true?

Surely it is morning, and in the mail the chainstore
people offer a new Fall line

there is a bill for union dues, a request for additional support
   then the news: somewhere a million men are on the march again, elsewhere the horror mounts, and there are incidental leprosies
      briefly, here, the recollection of some old, imagined splendor, to be quickly dropped and crushed completely out

Are there any questions?
   Has anyone any objections to make?
      Can a new political approach or a better private code evolve from this?
         Does it hold any premise based on faith alone?

Or are you, in fact, a privileged ghost returned, as usual, to haunt yourself?
   A vigorous, smiling corpse come back to tour the morgues?
      To inspect the scene of the invisible death, and then to report

And if to report, are there any different answers now, at last?

The Program

ACT ONE, Madrid-Barcelona, Time, the present
  ACT TWO, Paris in springtime, during the siege
    ACT THREE, London, Bank Holiday, after an air
    raid
      ACT FOUR, a short time later in the U.S.A.

EAT ZEPHYR CHOCOLATES
  (do not run for the exit in case of fire
  the Rome-Berlin Theater has no exits)
    SUZANNE BRASSIERES FOR PERFECT FORM

CAST, IN THE ORDER OF DISAPPEARANCE
  infants
    women and children
      soldiers, sailors, miscellaneous crowds

With 2,000 wounded and 1,000 dead
  10,000 wounded and 5,000 dead
    100,000 wounded and 50,000 dead
      10,000,000 wounded and 5,000,000 dead

(Scenes by Neville Chamberlain
  costumes, courtesy of Daladier
    Spanish Embargo by the U.S. Congress
      music and lighting by Pius XI)

SMOKE EL DEMOCRACIES
  TRY THE NEW GOLGOTHA FOR COCKTAILS AFTER THE
  SHOW.

American Rhapsody (5)

Tomorrow, yes, tomorrow
 there will suddenly be new success, like Easter
 clothes, and a strange and different fate
  and bona fide life will arrive at last, stepping from a
  nonstop monoplane with chromium doors and a
  silver wing and straight, white staring lights

There will be the sound of silvery thunder again to stifle
the insane silence
 a new, tremendous sound will shatter the final
 unspoken question and drown the last, mute, terrible
 reply
  rockets, rockets, Roman candles, flares, will burst
  in every corner of the night, to veil with snakes of
  silvery fire the nothingness that waits and waits
   there will be a bright, shimmering, silver veil
   stretched everywhere, tight, to hide the deep,
   black, empty, terrible bottom of the world where
   people fall who are alone, or dead

Sick or alone
 alone or poor
  weak, or mad, or doomed, or alone

Tomorrow, yes, tomorrow, surely we begin at last to live
 with lots and lots of laughter
  solid silver laughter
   laughter, with a few simple instructions, and a
   bona fide guarantee.

Portrait

The clear brown eyes, kindly and alert, with 20-20
vision, give confident regard to the passing world
through R. K. Lampert & Company lenses framed in
gold
    his soul, however, is all his own
        Arndt Brothers necktie and hat (with feather)
        supply a touch of youth

With his soul his own, he drives, chats and drives the
second and third bicuspids, lower right, replaced by
bridgework, while two incisors have porcelain crowns

(Render unto federal, state, and city Caesar, but not
unto time
    render nothing unto time until Amalgamated Death
    serves final notice, in proper form

The vault is ready
    the will has been drawn by Clagget, Clagget, Clagget
    & Brown
        the policies are adequate, Confidential's best,
        reimbursing for disability, partial or complete, with
        double indemnity should the end be a pure and
        simple accident)

Nothing unto time
    nothing unto change
        nothing unto fate

nothing unto you, and nothing unto me, or to
any other known or unknown party or parties,
living or deceased

But Mercury shoes, with special arch supports, take
much of the wear and tear
on the course, a custombuilt driver corrects a
tendency to slice
love's ravages have been repaired (it was a textbook
case) by Drs. Schultz, Lightner, Mannheim, and
Goode
while all of it is enclosed in excellent tweed, with
Mr. Baumer's personal attention to the shoulders
and the waist

And all of it now roving, chatting amiably through space
in a Plymouth 6
with his soul (his own) at peace, soothed by Walter
Lippmann, and sustained by Haig & Haig.

C Stands for Civilization

They are able, with science, to measure the millionth of
a millionth of an electron-volt
THE TWENTIETH CENTURY COMES BUT ONCE
the natives can take to caves in the hills, said the
British M.P., when we bomb their huts
THE TWENTIETH CENTURY COMES BUT ONCE

Electric razors,
   I am the law, said Mayor Hague
      the lynching was televised, we saw the whole thing
      from beginning to end, we heard the screams and
      the crackle of flames in a soundproof room
      THE TWENTIETH CENTURY COMES BUT ONCE

You are born but once
   you have your chance to live but once
      you go mad and put a bullet through your head but
      once

THE TWENTIETH CENTURY COMES BUT ONCE
   once too soon, and just a little too fast
      once too late and a little too slow, just once too
      often

But zooming through the night in Lockheed
monoplanes the witches bring pictures of the latest
disaster exactly on time
   THE TWENTIETH CENTURY COMES BUT ONCE
      ONLY ONCE, AND STAYS FOR BUT ONE HUNDRED
      YEARS.

Take a Letter

Would you like to live, yourself, the way that other
people do
    would you like to be the kind of man you've always
    dreamed you'd be
        do you know that tax consultants get very good pay
            or would you rather become a detective and trap
            your man

ARREST HIM, ARREST HIM
    how do you know you can't compose
        ARREST THAT MAN
            would you like to have poise, speak Russian,
            Spanish, French

ARREST THAT MAN, HE FITS THE DESCRIPTION
PERFECTLY
    maybe you, too, can paint
        I KNOW HIM FROM HIS PICTURE, IT WAS IN THE
        MORNING PAPERS
            want to stop the tobacco habit, like to study
            aviation, own a genuine diamond ring

I TELL YOU, IT'S HIM
    do you crawl with crazy urges
        get those wild, wild feelings that you can't control
            IT'S HIM, IT'S HIM, HE'S HERE AGAIN, HE'S
            WANTED, IT'S HIM

Feel a big, strange, jumpy, weird, crazy, new impulse
    want to own your own home and wear the very best
    clothes
        would you like to live and love and learn as other
        people do

STOP HIM, HE SOUNDS JUST EXACTLY LIKE THE MISSING
BOSTON HEIR
    HOLD HIM, HE MIGHT EVEN BE THE SENATOR FROM
    THE SOUTH WHOSE MIND WENT BLANKER STILL
        ARREST THAT MAN, HE FITS THE HUMAN PYTHON
        FROM A TO Z

But he never could be you
    the most impressive bankrupt at the most exclusive
    club
        or the mildest, coolest madman on the whole
        Eastern coast.

Radio Blues

    Try 5 on the dial, try 10, 15
just the ghost of an inch, did you know, divides Japan
            and Peru
20, 25
is that what you want, static and a speech and the
            fragment of a waltz, is that just right
or what do you want at twelve o'clock, with the visitors
            gone, and the Scotch running low

30, 35, 35 to 40 and 40 to 50
free samples of cocoa, and the Better Beer Trio, and
           hurricane effects for a shipwreck at sea
but is that just right to match the feeling that you have

From 60 to 70 the voice in your home may be a
           friend of yours
from 70 to 80 the voice in your home may have a
           purpose of its own
from 80 to 90 the voice in your home may bring you
           love, or war
but is that what you want

100, 200, 300, 400
would you like to tune in on the year before last
500, 600
or the decade after this, with the final results of the final
           madness and the final killing

600, 700, 800, 900
what program do you want at midnight, or at noon, at
           three in the morning
at 6 A.M. or at 6 P.M.
with the wind still rattling the windows, and shaking the
           blinds

Would you care to bring in the stations past the stars
would you care to tune in on your dead love's grave

1000, 2000, 3000, 4000
is that just right to match the feeling that you want

5000, 6000
is that just right
7000, 8000
is that what you want to match the feeling that you have
9000, 10,000
would you like to tune in upon your very own life, gone
somewhere far away.

Dance of the Mirrors

You
you at night and you in the sun
you, farther than the pylons that walk, charged with
light, across the fields of wheat and vanish
through the hills
you, invincible to change, and vulnerable to every wind
that breathes upon these singing wires
you, and the clouds above the wires, and the sky above
the hills

Yes, you
everywhere you, driving, laughing, arranging the day,
efficient at the desk and brisk across the phone
telegrams and you, cocktails and you
you and the image in the glass, and the knock at the
door, then the second image, and the embrace,
the kiss
you, yes
you beneath the sculptured slab and raised mound, lost
with the echo of Handel among cathedral beams

You, you
and all of the things that the world ignores, all of the
        things that the world has forgotten, all that the
        world will never know
you and the glow-worm, you and the rainbow, you and
        the desert mirage and the Northern Lights
you, the footstep, you, the drumbeat, you, the firedance,
        you, the whirlwind, you, the trigger, the bullet,
        the heart, and the shield.

Manhattan

(*To Alfred Hayes*)

Deep city
tall city, worn city, switchboard weaving what ghost
        horizons (who commands this cable, who escapes
        from this net, who shudders in this web), cold
        furnace in the sky
guardian of this man's youth, graveyard of the other's,
        jailer of mine
harassed city, city knowing and naive, gay in the
        theaters, wary in the offices, starved in the
        tenements
city ageless in the hospital delivery rooms and always
        too old, or too young, in the echoing morgues

City for sale, for rent
five rooms, the former tenant's mattress, still warm, is
        leaving on the van downstairs
move in

here are the keys to the mailbox, the apartment, and the
        outside door
it is yours, all yours, this city, this street, this house
        designed by a famous architect, you would know
        the name at once
this house where the suicide lived, perhaps this floor,
        this room that reflects the drugstore's neon light
here, where the Wall Street clerk, the engineer, the
        socialist, the music teacher all lived by turns
move in
move in, arrange the furniture and live, live, go in the
        morning to return at night
relax, plan, struggle, succeed, watch the snow fall and
        hear the rain beat, know the liner's voice, see the
        evening plane, a star among stars, go north at the
        scheduled hour
make so many phone calls in the foyer again, have so
        many business talks in the livingroom, there will
        be cocktails, cards, and the radio, adultery again
        (downtown), vomit (again) in the bath
scenes, hysterics, peace
live, live, live, live, and then move out
go with the worn cabinets and rugs all piled on the curb
        while the city passes and the incoming tenant
        (unknown to you) awaits
yes, go
but remember, remember that, remember that year, that
        season

   Do you, do you, do you
city within city, sealed fortress within fortress, island
        within enchanted island

do you, there outside the stationer's shop, still hear
	gun-fire and instant death on winter nights
still see, on bright Spring afternoons, a thin grey figure
	crumple to the walk in the park
(who stared, who shrugged and went home, who stayed
	and shivered while the ambulance arrived
let the spirit go free, ship the body west)
do you remember that, do you
do you remember the missing judge, the bigshot
	spender and the hundred dollar bills (did he do
	three years)
the ballgame of ballgames (the fourth in the series, or
	was that the sixth)
the reform party and the gambling cleanup (a ten-day
	laugh), the returning champion (what about it),
	the abortion (so what), the rape (who cares)
the paralyzed newsboy, the taxi-driver who studied
	dramatics, the honest counterman, the salesman
	in love with the aviator's wife, the day at the zoo,
	the evening in the park, the perfect girl, the
	funny little guy with the funny little face

	City, city, city
eye without vision, light without warmth, voice without
	mind, pulse without flesh
mirror and gateway, mirage, cloud against the sun
do you remember that, that year, that season, that day,
	that hour, that name, that face
do you remember

Only the day, fulfilled, as it burns in the million
        windows of the west
only the promise of the day, returning, as it flames on
        the roofs and spires and steeples of the east.

Scheherazade

Not the saga of your soul at grips with fate,
        bleedingheart, for we have troubles of our own
nor the inside story of the campaign scandal, wiseguy,
        for we were there ourselves, or else we have
        forgotten it years ago
not all the answers, oracle, to politics and life and love,
        you have them but your book is out of date
no, nor why you are not a heel, smooth baby, for that is
        a lie, nor why you had to become one, for that
        is much too true
nor the neighborhood doings five years ago, rosebud,
        nor the ruined childhood, nor the total story
        of friendship betrayed
nor how cynical you are, rumpot, and why you
        became so

Give us, instead, if you must, something that we can
        use, like a telephone number
or something we can understand, like a longshot tip on
        tomorrow's card
or something that we have never heard before, like the
        legend of Ruth.

How Do I Feel?

Get this straight, Joe, and don't get me wrong.
Sure, Steve, O.K., all I got to say is, when do I get the
        dough?

Will you listen for a minute? And just shut up? Let a
        guy explain?
Go ahead, go ahead, I won't say a word.

Will you just shut up?
O.K., I tell you, whatever you say, it's O.K. with me.

What's O.K. about it, if that's the way you feel?
What do you mean, how do I feel? What do you know,
        how I feel?

Listen, Joe, a child could understand, if you'll listen for
        a minute without butting in, and don't get so
        sore.
You got to collect it first before you lay it out, sure, I
        know, you can't be left on a limb yourself.

Me? On a limb? For a lousy fifty bucks?
Take it easy, Steve, I'm just saying

I'm just telling you
Wait, listen

Now listen, wait, will you listen for a minute? That's all
        I ask. Yes or no?
O.K., Steve, O.K.

O.K.?

O.K., O.K.

O.K., then, and you won't get sore?

O.K., Steve. All I got to say is, when do I get the dough?

FROM **The Agency**

AGENT NO. 174 RESIGNS

The subject was put to bed at midnight, and I picked
        him up again at 8 A.M.
I followed, as usual, while he made his morning rounds.
After him, and like him, I stepped into taxis, pressed
        elevator buttons, fed nickels into subway
        turnstiles, kept him under close surveillance
        while he dodged through heavy traffic and
        pushed through revolving doors.

We lunched very pleasantly, though separately, for
        $1.50, plus a quarter tip. (Unavoidable expense.)
Then we resumed. For twenty minutes on the corner
        the subject watched two shoeshine boys fish for a
        dime dropped through a subway grate. No dice.
And then on. We had a good stare into a window made
        of invisible glass.
Another hour in a newsreel movie—the usual famine,
        fashions, Florida bathing, and butchery. Then
        out again.
I realized, presently, that the subject was following a
        blonde dish in blue he had seen somewhere
        around.

(Nothing, ultimately, came of this.)
And shortly after that a small black pooch, obviously
lost, attached himself to your agent's heels.
Does he fit into this picture anywhere at all?
It doesn't matter. In any case, I resign.

Because the situation, awkward to begin with, swiftly
developed angles altogether too involved.
Our close-knit atomic world (night would disperse it)
woven of indifference (the blonde's), of love (the
subject's), of suspicion (my province), and of
forlorn hope (the dog's), this little world became
a social structure, and then a solar system with
dictates of its own.
We had our own world's fair in a pinball arcade. The
blonde had her picture taken in a photomat.
And so (whether by law, or by magnetism) did we.
But still there was nothing, in any of this, essentially
new to report.

Except, I began to think of all the things the subject
might have done, but he did not do.
All the exciting scenes he might have visited but failed
to visit, all the money I might have watched him
make or helped him spend, the murders he
might have committed, but somehow he
refrained.
What if he met a visiting star from the coast? And she
had a friend?
Or went to Havana, or the South Sea Isles?
Did my instructions, with expenses, cover the case?
But none of this happened. Therefore, I resign.

I resign, because I do not think this fellow knew what he
was doing.
I do not believe the subject knew, at all clearly, what he
was looking for, or from what escaping.
Whether from a poor man's destiny (relief and the
Bellevue morgue), or a middle-class fate (always
the same job with a different firm), or from a
Kreuger-Musica denouement.
And then, whose life am I really leading, mine or his?
His or the blonde's?

And finally because this was his business, all of it, not
mine.
Whatever conscience, boredom, or penal justice he
sought to escape, it was his business, not mine in
the least. I want no part of it.
I have no open or concealed passion for those doors we
opened together, those turnstiles we pushed,
those levers, handles, knobs.
Not for the shadow of a bathing beauty on a screen, nor
the picture of a ruined village. Nor any interest
in possible defects shown by invisible glass.

I mean, for instance, I do not (often) feel drawn toward
that particular type of blonde in that particular
shade of blue.
And I have no room to keep a dog.

Therefore, this resignation.
Whether signed in a Turkish bath, with a quart of rye,
or in a good hotel, sealed with a bullet, is none of
your business. None at all.

There is no law compelling any man on earth to do the
   same, second hand.
I am tired of following invisible lives down intangible
   avenues to fathomless ends.
Is this clear?
Herewith, therefore, to take effect at once, I resign.

PACT

It is written in the skyline of the city (you have seen it,
   that bold and accurate inscription), where the
   gray and gold and soot-black roofs project
   against the rising or the setting sun,
It is written in the ranges of the farthest mountains, and
   written by the lightning bolt,
Written, too, in the winding rivers of the prairies, and
   in the strangely familiar effigies of the clouds,

That there will be other days and remoter times, by far,
   than these, still more prodigious people and still
   less credible events,
When there will be a haze, as there is today, not quite
   blue and not quite purple, upon the river, a green
   mist upon the valley below, as now,

And we will build, upon that day, another hope (because
   these cities are young and strong),
And we will raise another dream (because these hills and
   fields are rich and green),

And we will fight for all of this again, and if need be
    again,
And on that day, and in that place, we will try again, and
    this time we shall win.

THE DOCTOR WILL SEE YOU NOW

This patient says he is troubled by insomnia, and that
    one finds it difficult to stay awake.
Miss A confides a fear of narrow places. Mr. B, in Wall
    Street, is everywhere pursued by a secret agent,
    and by a certain X-ray eye that transmits his
    business secrets to a rival clique.
Practice, in general, is good. The patients are of all
    classes. In every case the problem is to exorcise
    these devils. And to adjust.

To adjust the person to his gods, and to his own estate,
    and to the larger group.
Adjust to the conventions and the niceties. That is, by
    inference, to the Chamber of Commerce, to the
    local police, to the Society of Ancient
    Instruments, and to the West Side Bicycle Club.
Adjust the kleptomaniac to modes of safer intercourse.
    The bigamist to the canons of the church, and to
    the criminal code.
(And all of these, perhaps, to him.)
Adjust the devils to the saints. The saints to the smiling
    devils. The martyrs to the renegades, and each of
    them, alike, to the hearty fools.

Adjust to the present, and to a longer view.
To cities shining in the sky tonight, and smoking in the
        dust tomorrow.
Adjust the mothers. And the husbands. And the fathers.
        And the wives.
Adjust to the sons, once resolute, now dead. And to the
        daughters, living but mad.
Adjust to the morning crucifixion and the evening calm.
Adjust them all. And then adjust them to this new
        perspective. Adjust.

Mr. X believes the tall brunettes can bring him only
        grief. Mrs. Y walks backward to escape the evil
        eye. Mr. Z hears voices.
They have nothing new to communicate, but he is
        disturbed.

Madness, never obsolete, grows fashionable.
Do its canons, unlike those of any other pursuit, seem to
        make unreasonable demands upon the patient?
Or require of the practitioner, himself, adjustments too
        fantastic, perhaps too terrible to reach?

GENTLEMAN HOLDING HANDS WITH GIRL

Of you, both the known and unknown quantities, but
        more especially, of those unknown,
Of the mysteries of the arches and the ligaments, the
        question of the nerves and muscles, the haunting
        riddle of the joints,

Of jetblack eyes and nutbrown hair,
Of the latest movie star, and Hollywood, and of a job
that pays real dough, and then of debts, current
and past. The past?

Of the distant past. Of nutbrown eyes and jetblack hair.
Of blue eyes, and of yellow hair. Red hair and
hazel eyes. Gray eyes.
Of perfection: Can it ever be obtained?
Of time and change and chance. Right now, returning
from Arcturus, of you.

Of the crazy hats and negligee in the shops along the
avenue, of perfume and of lace;
A startling fragment abruptly, here, shoots to the surface
out of early youth;
Of Freud, and of Krafft-Ebing for a moment. Of
Havelock Ellis (must read, some day, in full).

Is it like stepping into a looking-glass, or like flying
through space?

Of the indubitable beginning of life, and of its
indubitable end,
Of the mirage within a mirage,
With all of the daughters of all the daughters summed
up, at last, in you.

PORTRAIT OF A COG

You have forgotten the monthly conference. Your four
        o'clock appointment waits in the ante-room. The
        uptown bureau is on the wire again.
Most of your correspondence is still unanswered, these
        bills have not been paid, and one of your trusted
        agents has suddenly resigned.
And where are this morning's reports? They must be
        filed at once, at once.

It is an hour you do not fully understand, a mood you
        have had so many times but cannot quite
        describe,
It is a fantastic situation repeated so often it is
        commonplace and dull,
It is an unlikely plot, a scheme, a conspiracy you helped
        to begin but do not, any longer, control at all.

Perhaps you are really in league with some maniac
        partner whom you have never met, whose voice
        you have never heard, whose name you do not
        even know.
It is a destiny that is yours, yours, all yours and only
        yours, a fate you have long ago disowned and
        disavowed.

When they dig you up, in a thousand years, they will
        find you in just this pose,
One hand upon the buzzer, the other reaching for the
        phone, eyes fixed upon the calendar, feet firmly
        on the office rug.

Shall you ask the operator for an outside wire? And then
      dictate this memo:
No (overwhelming) passions. No (remarkable) vices. No
      (memorable) virtues. No (terrific) motives.

Yes, when they dig you up, like this, a thousand years
      from now,
They will say: Just as he was in life. A man typical of the
      times, engaged in typical affairs.
Notice the features, especially, they will say. How self-
      assured they are, and how serene.

A LA CARTE

Some take to liquor, some turn to prayer,
Many prefer to dance, others to gamble, and a few
      resort to gas or the gun.
(Some are lucky, and some are not.)

Name your choice, any selection from one to twenty-
      five:
Music from Harlem? A Viennese waltz on the slot-
      machine phonograph at Jack's Bar & Grill? Or a
      Brahms Concerto over WXV?
(Many like it wild, others sweet.)

Champagne for supper, murder for breakfast, romance
      for lunch and terror for tea,

This is not the first time, nor will it be the last time the
      world has gone to hell.
(Some can take it, and some cannot.)

AMERICAN RHAPSODY (4)

First you bite your fingernails. And then you comb your
      hair again. And then you wait. And wait.
(They say, you know, that first you lie. And then you
      steal, they say. And then, they say, you kill.)

Then the doorbell rings. Then Peg drops in. And Bill.
      And Jane. And Doc.
And first you talk, and smoke, and hear the news and
      have a drink. Then you walk down the stairs.
And you dine, then, and go to a show after that,
      perhaps, and after that a night spot, and after
      that come home again, and climb the stairs
      again, and again go to bed.

But first Peg argues, and Doc replies. First you dance
      the same dance and you drink the same drink
      you always drank before.
And the piano builds a roof of notes above the world.
And the trumpet weaves a dome of music through
      space. And the drum makes a ceiling over
      space and time and night.
And then the table-wit. And then the check. Then home
      again to bed.
But first, the stairs.

And do you now, baby, as you climb the stairs, do you
still feel as you felt back there?
Do you feel again as you felt this morning? And the
night before? And then the night before that?

(They say, you know, that first you hear voices. And
then you have visions, they say. Then, they say,
you kick and scream and rave.)
Or do you feel: What is one more night in a lifetime of
nights?
What is one more death, or friendship, or divorce out of
two, or three? Or four? Or five?
One more face among so many, many faces, one more
life among so many million lives?

But first, baby, as you climb and count the stairs (and
they total the same) did you, sometime or
somewhere, have a different idea?
Is this, baby, what you were born to feel, and do, and
be?

YES, THE AGENCY CAN HANDLE THAT

You recommend that the motive, in Chapter 8, should
be changed from ambition to a desire, on the
heroine's part, for doing good; yes, that can be
done.
Installment 9 could be more optimistic, as you point
out, and it will not be hard to add a heartbreak to
the class reunion in Chapter 10.

Script 11 may have, as you say, too much political
        intrigue of the sordid type; perhaps a diamond-
        in-the-rough approach would take care of this.
        And 12 has a reference to war that, as you
        suggest, had better be removed; yes.
This brings us to the holidays, that coincide with our
        prison sequence. With the convicts' Christmas
        supper, if you approve, we can go to town.

Yes, this should not be difficult. It can be done. Why
        not?

And script 600 brings us to the millennium, with all the
        fiends of hell singing Bach chorales.
And in 601 we explore the Valleys of the Moon (why
        not?), finding in each of them fresh Fountains of
        Youth.

And there is no mortal ill that cannot be cured by a little
        money, or lots of love, or by a friendly smile; no.
And few human hopes go unrealized; no.
And the rain does not ever, anywhere, fall upon
        corroded monuments and the graves of the
        forgotten dead.

CLASS REUNION

And Steve, the athlete, where is he?
And Clark, the medico who played Chopin and quoted
        Keats, where is he now?

And Dale, who built that bridge (so often shown in the
      rotogravures) taming a veritable Styx on some
      fabulous continent?
Elvira, who dealt in nothing less than truths that were
      absolute?
And Henderson, law student who floated a financial
      empire, is it true he died in jail?

And true that Steve is bald, and broke, and fat?
And true that Dale's long bridge is a tangle of junk,
      destroyed by dynamite in a great retreat?

Perhaps the empire of credit was not, after all, so
      shrewd or bold.
Perhaps Clark did much better in drygoods, to tell the
      truth, than he would have with surgery or Keats.
Perhaps Dale's bridge was not, really, a towering
      miracle. Or it may be such miracles are not so
      important, after all.
It may be Elvira came as close to the thing, with her
      absolutes, as anyone else. She's the mother of
      five.

White mice, running mazes in behavior tests, have
      never displayed more cunning than these, who
      arrived by such devious routes at such incredible
      ends.

For it is the end, surely? We knew the story to be
      working toward an end, and this, then, is in fact
      the end?

And there is no chance we will be met tonight, or
   tomorrow night, or any other night, by destiny
   moving in still another direction?
As one might meet a figure on a dark street, and hear
   from the shadows a familiar but unwelcome
   voice:

"Hello, remember me? We had an appointment, but
   you broke it to attend a class reunion.
You can forget that, now. Tonight something new is
   coming up.
Let's go."

PAYDAY IN THE MORGUE

Go ahead, will you, see who's there, knocking at the
   door.
Knocking? Wasn't that a voice? Or the telephone
   ringing? Or a piano being played somewhere
   upstairs?

It may have been a voice, but there is no phone or piano
   in the place.
On the radio, I meant. A sort of a concert from very far
   away.

Radio? Where do you see any radio in here? Go ahead,
   will you, see who it is, we'll save the hand, and
   you can trust us with your chips.

I can, can I? How do I know I can? I never saw any of
      you people before tonight. Besides, how do I
      know whose is the body, and whose the voice? It
      might even be the future, and if it is, then what?

You would say that.
Well, it could be, couldn't it?

Don't mention that word. Don't even think the thought.
      Just answer the door.
Answer it yourself. These are the first decent cards I
      held all evening. Let them go ahead and knock.
      Some one, somewhere has to die, tonight, but
      some other person might be lucky as hell.

Maybe it's the wagon from the morgue, that's all,
      bringing somebody cold and dripping from the
      river, or bloody from the street. And that would
      be O.K., they were all square guys before the
      curtains went down.
Maybe it's Thunderbolt again, the Iroquois chief, with
      another message from some one long departed,
      and who's afraid of him?
Maybe they're the things Mr. Johnson's always seeing in
      dreams. Or a few of Mrs. Edwards' remote
      controls. Or the tiny bouncing men in Mr.
      Brown's DTs. And they aren't so bad, just crazy,
      that's all.

Yes, but wouldn't they come in by themselves, if it's
        them? Walls wouldn't stop them. Not a little
        wood, and stone, and steel.
Maybe we should ask. I guess we'd better.

Is that you, Mr. Johnson, in Coffin Compartment 404?
        Did you ring, Mrs. Edwards, in Compartment
        13? Are you haunted, Mr. Brown, by the torso
        murder baby? Are you haunted again by the man
        without a name?
Mr. Johnson? Mrs. Edwards? Mr. Brown? Mr. Brown?

They must be deaf in there. Deaf and blind. Deafer than
*   ashes and blinder than dust.*

Deafer than ashes, is that what I heard?
Did you hear those voices, did you hear them, too?
I wouldn't answer that, not if I were you. Like
        something straight from the Age of Ice.
Or something from the future like I said, didn't I say?

Now don't get excited. We'll just keep quiet and deal
        the cards and whoever it is they'll get tired and
        go away. How many for you?
One.
Two cards here, and I'm in with a dollar.
I'll just see that, and I raise you three.
Up another five.

Gentlemen, aren't the stakes a little too high, or is the sky the
*   limit?*

I'd answer the door, but you know how it is. A fellow
      with a family.
Sure.
It's either them or us, see what I mean?
Or you could put it like this, either them or some one
      else.
Either millions of men with feet like lizards and the
      heads of rats, or gods made of music bathed in
      blinding light.

LOVE, 20¢ THE FIRST QUARTER MILE

All right, I may have lied to you, and about you, and
      made a few pronouncements a bit too sweeping,
      perhaps, and possibly forgotten to tag the bases
      here or there,
And damned your extravagance, and maligned your
      tastes, and libeled your relatives, and slandered a
      few of your friends,
O.K.,
Nevertheless, come back.

Come home. I will agree to forget the statements that
      you issued so copiously to the neighbors and the
      press,
And you will forget that figment of your imagination,
      the blonde from Detroit;

I will agree that your lady friend who lives above us is
        not crazy, bats, nutty as they come, but on the
        contrary rather bright,
And you will concede that poor old Steinberg is neither
        a drunk, nor a swindler, but simply a guy, on the
        eccentric side, trying to get along.
(Are you listening, you bitch, and have you got this
        straight?)

Because I forgive you, yes, for everything,
I forgive you for being beautiful and generous and wise,
I forgive you, to put it simply, for being alive, and
        pardon you, in short, for being you.

Because tonight you are in my hair and eyes,
And every street light that our taxi passes shows me you
        again, still you,
And because tonight all other nights are black, all other
        hours are cold and far away, and now, this
        minute, the stars are very near and bright.

Come back. We will have a celebration to end all
        celebrations.
We will invite the undertaker who lives beneath us, and
        a couple of the boys from the office, and some
        other friends,
And Steinberg, who is off the wagon, by the way, and
        that insane woman who lives upstairs, and a few
        reporters, if anything should break.

Now, about that other one, the sober one
(To be objective, for a change, about one's public self.
      After all, each of us has that stupider side),
Yes, you have seen him around, that self-appointed Dr.
      Jekyll who shares (reluctantly) by day this name
      and being with his Mr. Hyde (as he would put it)
      of the night,

Yes, him,
That fellow with this face, this voice, and even (by some
      crashing magic we will not go into now)
      possessed with a few of the same superficial
      traits,
That one whose first awakening voice is a hoarse,
      barbaric blast (you know against whom), who
      damns the excess (however moderate), deplores
      the extravagance and winces (as he reaches for
      the aspirin) at the smallest memory,
That fellow with the curdled eyes and not quite steady
      hands (poor guy, he must be slipping), to say
      nothing of a disposition that is really a
      wonderful, wonderful thing in itself,

Yes, well, now that you have the picture, take him,
And all his pathetic protests and his monumental vows
      to abstain, totally, forthwith (these need not
      concern us here)
(Two more of the same)

But, more especially, his pious recantations and denials,
      his ceaseless libel of one who is (why dodge the
      issue?) his mental, physical, and yes, moral
      superior—
But do you begin to see the point?

Because the point is this (he talks of self-respect, and
      decency is a favorite word of his), the point is
      this:
Does he think that he is the only one?
Does he think that he is the only man on earth who has
      felt this thing?
The only person ever to sit and watch the rain drive
      against the lighted windows, revolving at once
      some private trouble and knowing, for
      everything that breathes, a cold impersonal
      dismay?

From which (drinking, he says, is just an escape) he
      searches daily, down a thousand familiar avenues,
      for an escape that simply does not exist
(Those Chinese dreams he palms as reality, those
      childish ambitions, and then that transparent
      guile of his),
That fool (who must, it seems, be suffered) (but not
      gladly), that bore (and who has tolerated most?
      Has overlooked most? Which of us has forgiven
      most), that fool in love with some frowsy fate
      that plays with him as a cat plays with a mouse,

That fool (and this, at last, is the question), what would
   his decency amount to, but for the simple
   decency of this escape?

And if this is not true,
If this is not the final truth, then no one here is drunk,
   drunk as a lord of ancient France,
If this is not the inescapable truth, then the night is not
   dark but bright as day, and the lights along the
   street are not really made of burning pearls and
   rubies dipped in liquid fire,
If this is not true, the truth itself, as hard as hell and
   stronger than death,
Then time does not fly but life grows younger by the
   hour, and the rain is not falling, falling,
   everywhere falling,
And there are not, here, only pleasant sights and sounds
   and a pleasant warmth.

READINGS, FORECASTS, PERSONAL GUIDANCE

It is not—I swear it by every fiery omen to be seen these
   nights in every quarter of the heavens, I affirm it
   by all the monstrous portents of the earth and of
   the sea—
It is not that my belief in the true and mystic science is
   shaken, nor that I have lost faith in the magic of
   the cards, or in the augury of dreams, or in the
   great and good divinity of the stars.

No, I know still whose science fits the promise to the
      inquirer's need, invariably, for a change: Mine.
      My science foretells the wished-for journey, the
      business adjustment, the handsome stranger.
      (Each of these is considered a decided change.)
And I know whose skill weighs matrimony, risks a flyer
      in steel or wheat against the vagaries of the
      moon.
(Planet of dreams, of mothers and of children, goddess
      of sailors and of all adventurers, forgive the
      liberty. But a man must eat.) My skill,
Mine, and the cunning and the patience. (Two dollars
      for the horoscope in brief and five for a twelve
      months' forecast in detail.)

No, it is this: The wonders that I have seen with my
      own eyes.

It is this: That still these people know, as I do not, that
      what has never been on earth before may still
      well come to pass,
That always, always there are new and brighter things
      beneath the sun,
That surely, in bargain basements or in walk-up flats, it
      must be so that still from time to time they hear
      wild angel voices speak.

It is this: That I have known them for what they are,
Seen thievery written plainly in their planets, found
      greed and murder and worse in their birth dates

and their numbers, guilt etched in every line of
every palm,
But still a light burns through the eyes they turn to me,
a need more moving than the damned and dirty
dollars (which I must take) that form the pattern
of their larger hopes and deeper fears.

And it comes to this: That always I feel another hand,
not mine, has drawn and turned the card to find
some incredible ace,
Always another word I did not write appears in the spirit
parchment prepared by me,
Always another face I do not know shows in the dream,
the crystal globe, or the flame.

And finally, this: Corrupt, in a world bankrupt and
corrupt, what have I got to do with these
miracles?
If they want miracles, let them consult some one else.
Would they, in extremity, ask them of a physician? Or
expect them, in desperation, of an attorney? Or
of a priest? Or of a poet?

Nevertheless, a man must eat.
Mrs. Raeburn is expected at five. She will communicate
with a number of friends and relatives long
deceased.

**AFTERNOON OF A PAWNBROKER
AND OTHER POEMS** | 1943

Continuous Performance

The place seems strange, more strange than ever, and
      the times are still more out of joint;
Perhaps there has been some slight mistake?

It is like arriving at the movies late, as usual, just as the
      story ends:
There is a carnival on the screen. It is a village in
      springtime, that much is clear. But why has the
      heroine suddenly slapped his face? And what
      does it mean, the sequence with the limousine
      and the packed valise? Very strange.
Then love wins. Fine. And it is the end. O.K.
But how do we reach that carnival again? And when will
      that springtime we saw return once more? How,
      and when?

Now, where a moment ago there was a village square,
      with trees and laughter, the story resumes itself
      in arctic regions among blinding snows. How
      can this be?
What began in the long and shining limousine seems
      closing now, fantastically, in a hansom cab.

The amorous business that ended with happiness
        forever after is starting all over again, this time
        with a curse and a pistol shot. It is not so good.

Nevertheless, though we know it all and cannot be
        fooled, though we know the end and nothing
        deceives us,
Nevertheless we shall stay and see what it meant, the
        mystery of the packed valise,
Why curses change at last to kisses and to laughter in a
        limousine (for this is fixed, believe me, fixed),
How simply and how swiftly arctic blizzards melt into
        blowing trees and a village fair.

And stay to see the Hydra's head cut off, and grown
        again, and incredibly multiplied,
And observe how Sisyphus fares when he has once more
        almost reached the top,
How Tantalus again will nearly eat and drink.

And learn how Alph the sacred river flows, in Xanadu,
        forever to a sunless sea,
How, from the robes of simple flesh, fate emerges from
        new and always more fantastic fate.

Until again we have the village scene. (And now we
        know the meaning of the packed valise)
And it is a carnival again. In spring.

Art Review

Recently displayed at the Times Square station, a new
        Vandyke on the face-cream girl.
(Artist unknown. Has promise, but lacks the brilliance
        shown by the great masters of the Elevated age)
The latest wood carving in a Whelan telephone booth,
        titled "O Mortal Fools WA 9-5090," shows two
        winged hearts above an ace of spades.
(His meaning is not entirely clear, but this man will go far)
A charcoal nude in the rear of Flatbush Ahearn's Bar &
        Grill, "Forward to the Brotherhood of Man," has
        been boldly conceived in the great tradition.
(We need more, much more of this)
Then there is the chalk portrait, on the walls of a
        waterfront warehouse, of a gentleman wearing a
        derby hat: "Bleecker Street Mike is a
        doublecrossing rat."
(Morbid, but powerful. Don't miss)

Know then by these presents, know all men by these
        signs and omens, by these simple thumbprints on
        the throat of time,
Know that Pete, the people's artist, is ever watchful,
That Tuxedo Jim has passed among us, and was much
        displeased, as always,
That George the Ghost (no man has ever seen him) and
        Billy the Bicep boy will neither bend nor break,
That Mr. Harkness of Sunnyside still hopes for the best,
        and has not lost his human touch,
That Phantom Phil, the master of them all, has come
        and gone, but will return, and all is well.

Cracked Record Blues

If you watch it long enough you can see the clock move,
If you try hard enough you can hold a little water in the
      palm of your hand,
If you listen once or twice you know it's not the needle,
      or the tune, but a crack in the record when
      sometimes a phonograph falters and repeats, and
      repeats, and repeats, and repeats—

And if you think about it long enough, long enough,
      long enough, long enough then everything is
      simple and you can understand the times,
You can see for yourself that the Hudson still flows, that
      the seasons change as ever, that love is always
      love,
Words still have a meaning, still clear and still the same;
You can count upon your fingers that two plus two still
      equals, still equals, still equals, still equals—
There is nothing in this world that should bother the
      mind.

Because the mind is a common sense affair filled with
      common sense answers to common sense facts,
It can add up, can add up, can add up, can add up
      earthquakes and subtract them from fires,
It can bisect an atom or analyze the planets—
All it has to do is to, do is to, do is to, do is to start at
      the beginning and continue to the end.

Travelogue in a Shooting-Gallery

There is a jungle, there is a jungle, there is a vast, vivid,
        wild, wild, marvelous, marvelous, marvelous
        jungle,
Open to the public during business hours,
A jungle not very far from an Automat, between a hat
        store there, and a radio shop.

There, there, whether it rains, or it snows, or it shines,
Under the hot, blazing, cloudless, tropical neon skies
        that the management always arranges there,
Rows and rows of marching ducks, dozens and dozens
        and dozens of ducks, move steadily along on
        smoothly-oiled ballbearing feet,
Ducks as big as telephone books, slow and fearless and
        out of this world,
While lines and lines of lions, lions, rabbits, panthers,
        elephants, crocodiles, zebras, apes,
Filled with jungle hunger and jungle rage and jungle
        love,
Stalk their prey on endless, endless rotary belts through
        never-ending forests, and burning deserts, and
        limitless veldts,
To the sound of tom-toms, equipped with silencers,
        beaten by thousands of savages hidden there.

And there it is that all the big game hunters go, there
        the traders and the explorers come,
Leanfaced men with windswept eyes who arrive by
        streetcar, auto or subway, taxi or on foot,
        streetcar or bus,

And they nod, and they say, and they need no more:
"There . . . there . . .
There they come, and there they go."

And weighing machines, in this civilized jungle, will
        read your soul like an open book, for a penny at a
        time, and tell you all,
There, there, where smoking is permitted,
In a jungle that lies, like a rainbow's end, at the very end
        of every trail,
There, in the only jungle in the whole wide world
        where ducks are waiting for streetcars,
And hunters can be psychoanalyzed, while they smoke
        and wait for ducks.

Thirteen O'Clock

Why do they whistle so loud, when they walk past the
        graveyard late at night?
Why do they look behind them when they reach the
        gates? Why do they have any gates? Why don't
        they go through the wall?
But why, O why do they make that horrible whistling
        sound?

GO AWAY, LIVE PEOPLE, STOP HAUNTING THE DEAD.

If they catch you, it is said, they make you rap, rap, rap
        on a table all night,

And blow through a trumpet and float around the room
      in long white veils,
While they ask you, and ask you: Can you hear us,
      Uncle Ted?
Are you happy, Uncle Ted? Should we buy or should we
      sell? Should we marry, Uncle Ted?
What became of Uncle Ned, Uncle Ted, and is he
      happy, and ask him if he knows what became of
      Uncle Fred?

KEEP AWAY, LIVE PEOPLE, KEEP FAR AWAY,
STAY IN THE WORLD'S OTHER WORLD WHERE YOU
      REALLY BELONG, YOU WILL PROBABLY BE MUCH
      HAPPIER THERE.

And who knows what they are hunting for, always
      looking, looking, looking with sharp bright eyes
      where they ought to have sockets?
Whoever saw them really grin with their teeth?
Who knows why they worry, or what they scheme, with
      a brain where there should be nothing but good,
      damp air?

STAY AWAY, LIVE PEOPLE, STAY AWAY, STAY AWAY,
YOU MEAN NO HARM, AND WE AREN'T AFRAID OF YOU,
      AND WE DON'T BELIEVE SUCH PEOPLE EXIST,
BUT WHAT ARE YOU LOOKING FOR? WHO DO YOU WANT?
WHO? WHO? WHO? O WHO?

Reception Good

Now, at a particular spot on the radio dial, "—in this
    corner, wearing purple trunks,"
Mingles, somehow, with the news that "—powerful
    enemy units have been surrounded in the
    drive—"
And both of these with the information that "—there is
    a way to avoid having chapped and roughened
    hands."

Such are the new and complex harmonies, it seems, of a
    strange and still more complex age;
It is not that the reception is confused or poor, but
    rather it is altogether too clear and good,

And no worse, in any case, than that other receiving set,
    the mind,
Forever faithfully transmitting the great and little
    impulses that arrive, however wavering or loud,
    from near and far:
"It is an ill wind—" it is apt to report, underscoring this
    with "—the bigger they are the harder they fall,"
    and simultaneously reminding, darkly, that
    "Things are seldom as they seem,"

Reconciling, with ease, the irreconcilable,
Piecing together fragments of a flashing past with
    clouded snapshots of the present and the future,
("Something old, something new," its irrelevant
    announcer states. "Something borrowed,
    something blue.")

Fashioning a raw, wild symphony of a wedding march, a
        drinking song, and a dirge,
Multiplying enormous figures with precision, then
        raising the question: But after all, what is a man?
Somehow creating hope and fresh courage out of
        ancient doubt.

"Both boys are on their feet, they're going to it," the
        radio reports,
"—the sinking was attended by a heavy loss of life—"
"—this amazing cream for quick, miraculous results."

How many pieces are there, in a simple jigsaw puzzle?
How many phases of a man's life can crowd their way
        into a single moment?
How many angels, actually, can dance on the point of a
        pin?

Confession Overheard in a Subway

You will ask how I came to be eavesdropping, in the first
        place.
The answer is, I was not.
The man who confessed to these several crimes (call
        him John Doe) spoke into my right ear on a
        crowded subway train, while the man whom he
        addressed (call him Richard Roe) stood at my
        left.

Thus, I stood between them, and they talked, or
     sometimes shouted, quite literally straight
     through me.
How could I help but overhear?
Perhaps I might have moved away to some other strap.
     But the aisles were full.
Besides, I felt, for some reason, curious.

"I do not deny my guilt," said John Doe. "My own, first,
     and after that my guilty knowledge of still
     further guilt.
I have counterfeited often, and successfully.
I have been guilty of ignorance, and talking with
     conviction. Of intolerable wisdom, and keeping
     silent.
Through carelessness, or cowardice, I have shortened
     the lives of better men. And the name for that is
     murder.
All my life I have been a receiver of stolen goods."

"Personally, I always mind my own business," said
     Richard Roe. "Sensible people don't get into
     those scrapes."

I was not the only one who overheard this confession.
Several businessmen, bound for home, and housewives
     and mechanics, were within easy earshot.
A policeman sitting in front of us did not lift his eyes, at
     the mention of murder, from his paper.
Why should I be the one to report these crimes?

You will understand why this letter to your paper is
anonymous. I will sign it: Public Spirited
Citizen, and hope that it cannot be traced.
But all the evidence, if there is any clamor for it, can be
substantiated.
I have heard the same confession many times since, in
different places.
And now that I think of it, I had heard it many times
before.

"Guilt," said John, "is always and everywhere nothing
less than guilt.
I have always, at all times, been a willing accomplice of
the crass and the crude.
I have overheard, daily, the smallest details of
conspiracies against the human race, vast in their
ultimate scope, and conspired, daily, to launch
my own.
You have heard of innocent men who died in the chair.
It was my greed that threw the switch.
I helped, and I do not deny it, to nail that guy to the
cross, and shall continue to help.
Look into my eyes, you can see the guilt.
Look at my face, my hair, my very clothing, you will see
guilt written plainly everywhere.
Guilt of the flesh. Of the soul. Of laughing, when others
do not. Of breathing and eating and sleeping.
I am guilty of what? Of guilt. Guilty of guilt, that is all,
and enough."

Richard Roe looked at his wristwatch and said: "We'll
　　　be twenty minutes late.
After dinner we might take in a show."

Now, who will bring John Doe to justice for his
　　　measureless crimes?
I do not, personally, wish to be involved.
Such nakedness of the soul belongs in some other
　　　province, probably the executioner's.
And who will bring the blunt and upright Richard Roe
　　　to the accuser's stand, where he belongs?
Or will he deny and deny his partnership?

I have done my duty, as a public spirited citizen, in any
　　　case.

King Juke

The juke-box has a big square face,
A majestic face, softly glowing with red and green and
　　　purple lights.
Have you got a face as bright as that?

BUT IT'S A PROVEN FACT, THAT A JUKE-BOX HAS NO EARS.

With its throat of brass, the juke-box eats live nickels
　　　raw;
It can turn itself on or shut itself off;

It has no hangovers, knows no regrets, and it never feels
the need for sleep.
Can you do that?
What can you do that a juke-box can't, and do it ten
times better than you?

And it hammers at your nerves, and stabs you through
the heart, and beats upon your soul—
But can you do that to the box?

Its resourceful mind, filled with thoughts that range
from love to grief, from the gutter to the stars,
from pole to pole,
Can seize its thoughts between fingers of steel,
Begin them at the start and follow them through in an
orderly fashion to the very end.
Can you do that?
And what can you say that a juke-box can't, and say it in
a clearer, louder voice than yours?
What have you got, a juke-box hasn't got?

Well, a juke-box has no ears, they say.
The box, it is believed, cannot even hear itself.
IT SIMPLY HAS NO EARS AT ALL.

Elegy in a Theatrical Warehouse

They have laid the penthouse scenes away, after a truly
      phenomenal run,
And taken apart the courtroom, and the bright, shiny
        office, and laid them all away with the cabin in
        the clearing where the sun slowly rose through a
        smashing third act,
And the old family mansion on the road above the mill
      has been gone a long time,
And the road is gone—
The road that never did lead to any mill at all.

The telephone is gone, the phone that rang and rang,
      and never did connect with any other phone,
And the great steel safe where no diamonds ever were,
They have taken down the pictures, portraits of
        ancestors lost and unclaimed, that hung on the
        massive walls,
And taken away the books that reached to the study
      ceiling,
The rows and rows of books bound in leather and gold
      with nothing, nothing, nothing inside—

And the bureaus, and the chests, that were empty to the
      brim,
And the pistols that brought down so many, many
      curtains with so many, many blanks—

Almost everything is gone,
Everything that never held a single thing at all.

Piano Tuner

It is the sound of a cat like no cat ever seen before
         walking back and forth on ivory keys;
No note on this board, however the wires are tightened,
         can be tuned to any other note;
The instrument cannot be played, not correctly,
Not by any players known today, not from the scores
         and arrangements that now exist—

Somehow this wire, however strung, always returns a
         sound with an overtone, and always in the
         overtone the sound of distant gunfire can be
         plainly heard,
Another, however loose or taut, echoes as though to
         fingers tapping not music but bulletins
         despatched from remote time and space,
Then there are chords, neither minor chords nor
         discords, in some way filled with a major
         silence—

And it cannot be, it is not according to the standard
         scale;
Some wholly new and different kind of scale, perhaps,
         with unknown values, or no values, or values
         measured by chance and change—

This key responds with something not even sound at all,
         sometimes a feeling, and the feeling is anguish,
Sometimes a sense, like the touch of a hand,
Or a glimpse of familiar rooftops wrapped first in
         summer sunlight and then in falling snow—

As though the instrument were devil'd by melodies not
      written yet,
Or possessed by players not yet born.

Model for a Biography

Years in sporting goods, rich in experience, were
      followed by years in soda, candy, and cigars.
(If there is some connection, you might point it out
      here)
A real estate venture, resulting in ruin, prepared this
      man for his later triumph in the hardware game.
(If there is no connection, or if the logic seems weak, his
      is not the first life that failed to make sense—
You had better play it safe, and stick to one point):

HE WAS EXPERIENCED. HE WAS PREPARED.

And years of marriage (a happy, happy marriage)
      prepared him for years and years of divorce.
(O happy divorce)
(But you'd better not say that. Think of the relatives.
      And the public, by and large, would not believe
      you, or if they did, would not understand)
Then what can you say? You have to say something that
      makes a little sense:

HE WAS EXPERIENCED. HE WAS PREPARED.

He was kind, without fail, to other people's mothers;
Reprieved from insurance, he was sentenced to a bank,
    but made a daring, spectacular daylight escape;
Rejected by the Marines, he was welcomed by the
    Quartermaster Corps with open arms,
And when it is over, well, when it is over:

HE WILL BE EXPERIENCED. HE WILL BE PREPARED.

End of the Seers' Convention

We were walking and talking on the roof of the world,
In an age that seemed, at that time, an extremely
    modern age
Considering a merger, last on the agenda, of the Seven
    Great Leagues that held the Seven True Keys to
    the Seven Ultimate Spheres of all moral,
    financial, and occult life.

"I foresee a day," said one of the delegates, an astro-
    analyst from Idaho, "when men will fly through
    the air, and talk across space;
They will sail in ships that float beneath the water;
They will emanate shadows of themselves upon a
    screen, and the shadows will move, and talk, and
    seem as though real."

"Very interesting, indeed," declared a Gypsy delegate.
"But I should like to ask, as a simple reader of tea-leaves
    and palms:

How does this combat the widespread and growing evil
of the police?"

The astrologer shrugged, and an accidental meteor fell
from his robes and smoldered on the floor.
"In addition," he said, "I foresee a war,
And a victory after that one, and after the victory, a war
again."

"Trite," was the comment of a crystal-gazer from Miami
Beach.
"Any damn fool, at any damn time, can visualize wars,
and more wars, and famines and plagues.
The real question is: How to seize power from
entrenched and organized men of Common
Sense?"

"I foresee a day," said the Idaho astrologer, "when
human beings will live on top of flag-poles,
And dance, at some profit, for weeks and months
without any rest,
And some will die very happily of eating watermelons,
and nails, and cherry pies."

"Why," said a bored numerologist, reaching for his hat,
"can't these star-gazers keep their feet on the
ground?"
"Even if it's true," said a Bombay illusionist, "it is not,
like the rope-trick, altogether practical."

"And furthermore, and finally," shouted the astrologer,
  with comets and halfmoons dropping from his
  pockets, and his agitated sleeves,
"I prophesy an age of triumph for laziness and sleep,
  and dreams and utter peace.
I can see couples walking through the public parks in
  love, and those who do not are wanted by the
  sheriff.
I see men fishing beside quiet streams, and those who
  do not are pursued by collectors, and plastered
  with liens."

"This does not tell us how to fight against skepticism,"
  muttered a puzzled mesmerist, groping for the
  door.
"I think," agreed a lady who interpreted the cards, "we
  are all inclined to accept too much on faith."

A sprinkling of rain, or dragon's blood,
Or a handful of cinders fell on the small, black
  umbrellas they raised against the sky.

The Joys of Being a Businessman

Enter the proprietor of the Riviera Cafe;
Remarks, "It is a wonderful morning," as in fact it
  always is, for him;
Glances at the cash-register with marked disinterest,
  first, then at the morning man behind the bar,
  and at the early customers in front;

Disappears into the kitchen and at once returns, hangs
   up his coat;
Straightens the service flag in the window, and tests a
   Venetian blind;
States: "I was looking at the bills since ten o'clock,
   already;" (it is now about 11 A.M.)
Picks up a frond of palm leaves from the vase inside the
   door and inspects the stem, the leaves, the veins
   of the leaves;
Drinks coffee at the bar, peering steadily through the
   window at the street;
Queries, "Joe been here, yet?" And listens to the answer,
   Joe has not.

Puts on his coat and departs for a shave, returns, hangs
   up his coat;
Asserts: "Hot today. Another scorcher."
Studies the menu, frowns, shrugs in executive
   resignation, and puts it down; no comment;
Has a glass of vermouth on the stroke of noon.

Declares: "Tell Joe I'll be back tonight," and puts on his
   coat;
Gives a final, disapproving survey, filled with the cares
   of the High Command;
Austerely, but forgivingly departs.

Public Life

Then enter again, through a strange door, into a life
       again all strange,
Enter as a rich man, or perhaps a poor man,
Enter as beggarman or thief, doctor or lawyer or
       merchant or chief,
Enter, smiling, enter on tiptoe, enter blowing kisses,
       enter in tears,

But enter, enter,
Enter in overalls, mittens, sweater and cap, grime and
       grit and grease and gear,
Exit, then, exit and change, quick change and return,
Return in spats and pinstripe trousers, white bow tie
       and high silk hat, studs and tails,

Return as the villain: "The mortgage is due." (A role
       you never thought would be yours)
Enter as Nell (this comes with a shock): "You cur, you
       fiend."
Enter the hero: "Gold is your God and may he serve
       you well." (Can it possibly be this is you again?)

Enter Pa and Ma, strangers, stragglers, a miscellaneous
       crowd.
Enter Jane disguised as Du Barry, exit Du Barry
       disguised as Jane,
Come in with gun and mask and murderous intent,
Leave with bloodless hands and a silent prayer, in peace,

Exit to thunder and lightning and clouds and the night,
Enter on the following morning in sunshine, to the
      sound of birds,

Enter again to a different scene,
Enter again, through a strange door, into a life again all
      new and strange.

A Tribute, and a Nightmare

You wonder, sometimes, but more often worry, and feel
      dismayed in a world of change,
Seeing landmarks vanish, old bastions fall, and you
      frequently question what Fate may have in store
      for you—
But you really need not—
Whatever else it holds, it holds the changeless and
      eternal Martin Dies.

Will the world be bright, and filled with laughter?
You will hear all about it from Congressman Dies
      (Chairman of the Committee to Investigate
      Gloom).

Will the world be grim, inhabited by wolves with long,
      sharp teeth?
It will not go unchampioned. See Martin Dies,
      President of the Anti-Grandma League.

Will the people of the earth be nudists, eventually, and
      largely vegetarian?
Be especially wary of Dies, Martin, spinach crusader, the
      Kiddies' Kandidate unanimously acclaimed by
      Martin Dies.
Will the planet be Red with revolution (you hope) from
      the tropics to the poles?
You will have to deal (you fear, and rightly) with
      Commissar Dies, Chairman of the Committee to
      Probe Versive Activity.

Stranger, whoever you are, and whatever your final
      destination may be,
I give you, freely, a name to conjure with:
In heaven: Martin Dies, Chairman of the Membership
      Committee,
In hell: Martin Dies, President of United Coke & Coal.

Afternoon of a Pawnbroker

Still they bring me diamonds, diamonds, always
      diamonds,
Why don't they pledge something else for a change, if
      they must have loans, other than those diamond
      clasps and diamond rings,
Rubies, sapphires, emeralds, pearls,
Ermine wraps, silks and satins, solid gold watches and
      silver plate and violins two hundred years old,

And then again diamonds, diamonds, the neighborhood
    diamonds I have seen so many times before, and
    shall see so many times again?

Still I remember the strange afternoon (it was a season
    of extraordinary days and nights) when the first
    of the strange customers appeared,
And he waited, politely, while Mrs. Nunzio redeemed
    her furs, then he stepped to the counter and he
    laid down a thing that looked like a trumpet,
In fact, it was a trumpet, not mounted with diamonds,
    not plated with gold or even silver, and I started
    to say: "We can't use trumpets—"
But a light was in his eyes,
And after he was gone, I had the trumpet. And I stored
    it away. And the name on my books was Gabriel.

It should be made clear my accounts are always open to
    the police, I have nothing to conceal,
I belong, myself, to the Sounder Business Principles
    League,
Have two married daughters, one of them in Brooklyn,
    the other in Cleveland,
And nothing like this had ever happened before.
How can I account for my lapse of mind?
All I can say is, it did not seem strange. Not at the time.
    Not in that neighborhood. And not in that year.

And the next to appear was a man with a soft, persuasive
    voice,
And a kindly face, and the most honest eyes I have ever
    seen, and ears like arrows, and a pointed beard,

And what he said, after Mrs. Case had pledged her
      diamond ring and gone, I cannot now entirely
      recall,
But when he went away I found I had an apple. An
      apple, just an apple.
"It's been bitten," I remember that I tried to argue. But
      he smiled, and said in his quiet voice: "Yes, but
      only once."
And the strangest thing is, it did not seem strange. Not
      strange at all.

And still those names are on my books.
And still I see listed, side by side, those incongruous,
      and not very sound securities:
(1) Aladdin's lamp (I must have been mad), (1) Pandora's
      box, (1) Magic carpet,
(1) Fountain of youth (in good condition), (1) Holy
      Grail, (1) Invisible man (the only article never
      redeemed, and I cannot locate him), and others,
      others, many others,
And still I recall how my storage vaults hummed and
      crackled, from time to time, or sounded with
      music, or shot forth flame,
And I wonder, still, that the season did not seem one of
      unusual wonder, not even different—not at the
      time.

And still I think, at intervals, why didn't I, when the
      chance was mine, drink just once from that
      Fountain of youth?
Why didn't I open that box of Pandora?

And what if Mr. Gabriel, who redeemed his pledge and
went away, should some day decide to blow on
his trumpet?
Just one short blast, in the middle of some busy
afternoon?

But here comes Mr. Barrington, to pawn his
Stradivarius.
And here comes Mrs. Case, to redeem her diamond
ring.

STRANGER AT CONEY ISLAND
AND OTHER POEMS | 1948

Stranger at Coney Island

Not here, but a little farther, after we have passed
        through the hall of mirrors,
Seeing ourselves as ogres, devils, zombies, diplomats,
And after we have entered the dragon's jaws, drifting in
        our wooden boat down a silent river between
        white, gaping, enormous teeth,
Floating in darkness through grottos of ogres, then
        plastic devils stoking the painted flames of a
        gospel hell,
Coming safely again into sunlight, and the sound of a
        band—

To a cavern of echoes, where we hear the fun as
        strangers rehearse and rehearse the surprise they
        shall give themselves tomorrow,
Watch the signs flash red, and gold, and blue, and
        green,
"Eat" "Drink" "Be Merry" "At Mike's,"
Where there is no score, in any game, less than a
        million magic bells and a billion electric lights—

Beyond the highest peak of the steepest roller-coaster,
        in the company of persons we do not know,

Through arcades where anyone, even hermits, can have
     their fortunes told by iron gypsies sealed behind
     plateglass walls,
Into and beyond the bazaars where every prize is
     offered, dolls and vases, clocks and pillows,
     miniature closets for the family skeleton,
Given freely, with no questions asked, to any, any
     winner at all—

Until we emerge, safe at last, upon that broad and
     crowded beach,
To cry aloud: Is there a stranger here?
The stranger we have come so far, and through so many
     dangers, to find?
That one who, alone, can solve these many riddles we
     have found so difficult:—

Who, among us all, is the most popular person?
Whom shall we vote the handsomest, the wittiest, most
     likely to succeed?
What is the name, and the mission, of the embryo so
     long preserved in a jar of alcohol?
How may we ever distinguish between an honest, and a
     criminal face?—

Is this stranger somewhere among you?
Perhaps sprawled beneath a striped umbrella, asleep in
     the sand, or tossing a rubber ball to a child,
Or even now awaiting us, aware of our needs, knowing
     the very day and the hour.

4 A.M.

It is early evening, still, in Honolulu, and in London,
      now, it must be well past dawn,
But here in the Riviera Café, on a street that has been
      lost and forgotten long ago, as the clock moves
      steadily toward closing time,
The spark of life is very low, if it burns at all—

And here we are, four lost and forgotten customers in
      this place that surely will never again be found,
Sitting, at ten-foot intervals, along this lost and
      forgotten bar
(Wishing the space were further still, for we are still too
      close for comfort),
Knowing that the bartender, and the elk's head, and the
      picture of some forgotten champion
(All gazing at something of interest beyond us and
      behind us, but very far away),
Must somehow be aware of us, too, as we stare at the
      cold interior of our lives reflected in the mirror
      beneath and in back of them—

Hear how lonely the radio is, as its voice talks on and
      on, unanswered,
How its music proves again that one's life is either too
      humdrum or too exciting, too empty or too full,
      too this, too that;
Only the cat that has been sleeping in the window, now
      yawning and stretching and trotting to the
      kitchen to sleep again,

Only this living toy knows what we feel, knows what we
　　are, really knows what we merely think we
　　know—

And soon, too soon, it will be closing time, the door will
　　be locked,
Leaving each of us alone, then, with something too
　　ravaging for a name
(Our golden, glorious futures, perhaps)—

Lock the door now and put out the lights, before some
　　terrible stranger enters and puts, to each of us, a
　　question that must be answered with the truth—

They say the Matterhorn at dawn, and the Northern
　　Lights of the Arctic, are things that should be
　　seen;
They say, they say—in time, you will hear them say
　　anything, and everything;
What would the elk's head, or the remote bartender say,
　　if they could speak?
The booth where last night's love affair began, the spot
　　where last year's homicide occurred, are empty
　　now, and still.

Castaway

I know your neckties where they line the rack, orderly
        from day to day, from year to year,
And the clothing, except for the suit you wear,
        unwrinkled on the hangers, with each thing
        perfect in its perfect place—

O CASTAWAY, BEWARE—

You, a trifle anxious in this impersonal place, a little
        worried in these fiery times, but holding securely
        to your solid reef,
Certain you will arise upon the morning as strong and
        young as you are today—

O CASTAWAY, O CASTAWAY—

Send messages now, press many buttons and make
        phone calls, seek the best advice and speed, speed
        the telegrams for aid,
You do not want to meet the same fate as those others
        who have been cast out, and cast so far away—

Not one of those marooned here in some quiet office,
        park, or decent hotel,
The dreamers, or those too careful, the silent, or one of
        those who abruptly shouts aloud on some busy
        street,
Anarchist and time-server, timid and self-assured
        alike—

Each showing in his eyes, in the way he flexes his
        fingers, in the very way he speaks,
Each proving that he also recalls,
Remembers how the elders were all abandoned here,
        and knows that the young may fail in confusion,
        too—

Therefore, while the long sun rises, and still there is no
        sign,
But before the pale sun sets again, and then it will be
        too late—

O CASTAWAY, O CASTAWAY, O CASTAWAY, BEWARE.

The Juke-Box Spoke and the Juke-Box Said:

A few of them, sometimes, choose record number 9,
Or sometimes number 12,
And once in a while someone likes selection 5,
But the voice they really crave, all of them, everywhere
        and always, from the hour the doors open until
        the hour they close,
Repeated and repeated like a beating human heart,
Echoing in the walls, the ceiling, shaking the tables, the
        chairs, the floor—

OVER AND OVER, IT IS SELECTION NUMBER 8—

Whispered and chuckling, as though it arose from the
        bottom of the earth,

Or sometimes exploding like thunder in the room,
Not quite a curse and not exactly a prayer,
Eternally the same, but different, different, different
        every time—

THE WORDS OF NUMBER 8, THE MELODY OF NUMBER 8,
        THE SOUL OF NUMBER 8

Saying the simple thing they cannot say themselves,
Again and again, voicing the secret that they must
        reveal, and can never tell enough,
Yet it never quite gets told—
Sometimes number 9, or 12,
Or 5—

BUT ALWAYS NUMBER 8, AND ONCE AGAIN NUMBER 8,
TIME AFTER TIME, JUST ONCE MORE NUMBER
        8 . . . 8 . . . 8 . . .

Newspaperman

This charge was laid upon me long ago: Do not forget;
Remember these lives, that the world in turn will not
        forget—

Big John Marino, the terror of his district,
Where none were as strong as he, none as handsome, as
        cunning, as cruel,
Saying, before the state destroyed him:

"Tell them the truth. Tell them everything, so they will
        always know."
Know always, therefore, the great, the ruthless and
        bold, the one and only Big John—

Do not forget the fabulous bankrupt, and the vivid
        fortunes that somewhere, surely, the years still
        guard;
Keep the memory of an heiress, flashlit favorite in a
        season that cannot fade;
Never let fade, altogether, the programs identifying
        those others, miscellaneous members of the
        cast—

Each of them unique, though now the names, faces, and
        stories are obscured,
Each saying in words, or underneath the words, and
        some with their sealed eyes and cold lips
(But even so they were sure of themselves, still sure)
Urging always: "It is vital;
You must remember the fateful beginning, fully to
        understand the end
(Though of course there can be no real end);
To grasp the motives, fully, it is vital to remember the
        stamp of the mind,
Vital to know even the twist of the mind. . . ."

You will remember me?
Do not forget a newspaperman who kept his word

Bryce & Tomlins

Every need analyzed, each personal problem weighed,
    carefully, and solved according to the
    circumstance of each
(No investment too great. No question too small)
In confidence, at no cost, embarrassment, or obligation
    to you—

Offering maximum safety
(At 5%)
Full protection against change and chance, rust, moths,
    and the erratic flesh
(Trusts in perpetuity. Impartial executors of long-range
    wills)
Year after year, security in spite of the treacherous
    currents of impulse, yours and others',
Despite the swiftest tide of affairs—

Rails, chemicals, utilities, steel,
Listed or unlisted, let these stand guard through the
    shadowy times to be,
The heavy parchment with its exact phrases proof you
    shall walk this day's path, identically, tomorrow,
That as long as you wish you may see these streets and
    parks with the same eyes,
The same mood as today—

As though your features, yours, were stamped on the
    wind, yet more lasting than bronze,
The voice, free as always, yet recorded forever,

Your being, yours, still with its problems stronger than
even the chemicals or the steel—
Decades of experience behind each portfolio can protect
that future,
Filled with its unfinished business, incomplete desire,
and still with the stubborn will to protect that
future—

All of this, plus 5% of this, until the end of time.

Sherlock Spends a Day in the Country

The crime, if there was a crime, has not been reported
as yet;
The plot, if that is what it was, is still a secret
somewhere in this wilderness of newly fallen
snow;
The conference, if it was a conference, has been
adjourned, and now there is nothing in this scene
but pine trees, and silence, and snow, and still
more snow.

Nevertheless, in spite of all this apparent emptiness,
notice the snow;
Observe how it literally crawls with a hundred different
signatures of unmistakable life.
Here is a delicate, exactly repeated pattern, where,
seemingly, a cobweb came and went,

And here some party, perhaps an acrobat, walked
        through these woods at midnight on his
        mittened hands.
Thimbles, and dice tracks, and half moons, these
        trademarks lead everywhere into the hills;
The signs prove some amazing fellow on a bicycle rode
        straight up the face of a twenty-foot drift,
And someone, it does not matter who, walked steadily
        somewhere on obviously cloven feet.

Let us ourselves adjourn to the village bar, Watson (not
        saying very much when we get there),
To consider this mighty, diversified army, and what
        grand conspiracy of conspiracies it hatched,
What conclusions it reached, and where it intends to
        strike, and when,
Being careful to notice, as we go and return, the
        character and number of our own tracks in the
        snow.

Mrs. Fanchier at the Movies

If I could reply, but once, to these many new and kindly
        companions I have found
(Now that so many of the old are gone, so far and for so
        long)
Overhearing them on the radio or the phonograph, or
        here in the motion pictures, as now—

These electrical voices, so sure in the sympathy they
        extend,
Offering it richly through the long hours of the day and
        the longer hours of the night
(Closer at hand, and although automatic, somehow
        more understanding than a live friend)
Speaking sometimes to each other, but often straight at
        me—

Wishing I could reply, if only once,
Add somehow to the final burst of triumphant music, or
        even in tragedy mingle with the promise of the
        fading clouds—

But wondering, too, what it really was I at one time felt
        so deeply for,
The actual voice, or this muted thunder? These giant
        shadows, or the naked face?
Or something within the voice and behind the face?—

And wondering whether, now, I would have the courage
        to reply, in fact,
Or any longer know the words, or even find the voice.

The People v. The People

I have never seen him, this invisible member of the
        panel, this thirteenth juror, but I have certain
        clues;

I know, after so many years of practice, though I cannot
      prove I know;
It is enough to say, I know that I know.

He is five feet nine or ten, with piercing, bright,
      triumphant eyes;
He needs glasses, which he will not wear, and he is
      almost certainly stone deaf.
(Cf. Blair v. Gregg, which he utterly ruined.)
He is the juror forever looking out of the window,
      secretly smiling, when you make your telling
      point.
The one who is wide awake when you think he is asleep.
      The man who naps with his eyes wide open.
Those same triumphant eyes.
He is the man who knows. And knows that he knows.

His hair is meager and he wears wash ties, but these are
      not important points.
He likes the legal atmosphere, that is plain, because he
      is always there.
It is the decent, the orderly procedure that he likes.
He is the juror who arrived first, though you thought he
      was late; the one who failed to return from
      lunch, though you had not noticed.
Let me put it like this: He is the cause of your vague
      uneasiness when you glance about and see that
      the other twelve are all right.

I would know him if I were to see him, I could swear to
      his identity, if I actually saw him once;

I nearly overhead him, when I was for the defense:
    "They never indict anyone unless they are
    guilty;"
And when I was the State: "A poor man (or a rich man)
    doesn't stand a chance."
Always, before the trial's end, he wants to know if the
    sergeant knew the moon was full on that
    particular night.

And none of this matters, except I am convinced he is
    the unseen juror bribed, bought, and planted by
    The People,
An enemy of reason and precedent, a friend of illogic,
Something, I now know, that I know that I really
    know—

And he or anyone else is welcome to my Blackstone, or
    my crowded shelves of standard books,
In exchange for the monumental works I am convinced
    he has been writing through the years:
"The Rules of Hearsay;" "The Laws of Rumor;"
"An Omnibus Guide to Chance and Superstition," by
    One Who Knows.

Irene Has a Mind of Her Own

In the small but crowded attic of Irene's mind there is
    room for everything except confusion, hesitancy,
    and doubt;

Breath-control was the issue for one whole day, last
week
("Nobody recognized the food value of vegetable-tops,
either, ten years ago")—

And to this attic, like a bird building a nest with bits of
yarn, cardboard, and fragments of *The Reader's
Digest,*
She brings ancient leaflets and modern radio hints,
suggestions from strangers met on the train to
Buffalo, volumes legally filched from the public
library, telegrams intuitively received from the
great beyond:
"Your Troubles—How to Enjoy Them," "The Power of
Silence," "Ten Basic Errors of Contract
Bridge"—

The neighboring artist is a guaranteed immortal
("Van Gogh was even more insane"),
While extra-sensory perception is already an
indisputable fact
(The man who found Irene's purse returned her driver's
license),
And the richest part of any food, Irene knows, is the
natural skin in which it comes—

We, personally, no longer feel sure,
But looking at the paper in which the butter came, at
the empty tins and bottles we are saving
(Just in case),
We only know, and give profound thanks, that Irene is
on our side.

Minutes From the Chamber of Commerce

Ten divisions of bacillus Z stand poised at strategic
      points along the last frontier,
Fully trained and equipped,
And we face the future with confidence—

PROVIDED THE FUTURE DOES NOT COME TODAY—

Another vintage ancestor has been dug up in Crete,
      thirty ruined cities beneath the ruins on top,
The archeologists are digging, still,
And we in this city are prepared to take whatever fate
      may offer—

PROVIDED THE OFFER IS SOUND—

We know that voice-recorders have been attached to the
      phones of certain business rivals,
We have heard a rumor there may be thought-
      recorders, too,
Whatever the facts, we look them squarely, calmly,
      soberly in the face—

BUT ONLY WITH A TALL, COLD DRINK OF RYE IN HAND.

This Day

Now, in this moment that has no identical twin
        throughout all time,
Being yours, yours alone,
Intimate as the code engraved upon your fingertips, and
        as rare—

Marked as your own features, personal as the voice in
        which you conduct your daily affairs,
Complex as those affairs, growing always into a new and
        still more special crisis
(In each of which you have your particular skill at
        reading the omens and the signs),
Here, in this natural scene, in a numbered house on a
        street with a name—

Unique as the signature you find upon some letter you
        had long ago forgotten and mislaid,
Elusive as the mood that letter now recalls, the story
        and its end as briefly alive,
And now as wholly lost—

As though this long but crowded day, itself, could
        sometime fade,
Had in fact already slipped through the fingers and now
        were gone, gone, simply gone—

Leaving no one, least of all yourself, to enact the
        unfinished drama that you, alone, once knew so
        well,

No one to complete the triumph, to understand or even
        believe in the disaster that must be repaired,
No one to glimpse this plan that seemed, at one time,
        must, must, must be fulfilled.

Long Journey

With us, on this journey that begins in the green and
        chilly suburbs on a late Spring afternoon
(Rain streaking the windows of the bus)
And in addition to the passengers, the driver confidently
        seated at the wheel—

Goes Captain Wonder of "Macabre Comics," silently
        plunging through infinities of time and space,
        changing at will from man to God
(The young and cynical student of this magic, though
        spellbound, does not really believe)
Everywhere combating evil, at all times fearless, and
        never, for very long, deceived—

While an immortal of the diamond once more rounds
        third base for home,
Jogging easily at the side of one who hears neither the
        wet tires nor the exhaust,
Only the roar of thousands across a sunswept field—

And this, for another, is not an abandoned development
        we are passing now,
A place of ruined mansions and bypassed factories,

It is a giant hall of radio, filled with the instant laughter
         that follows every perfect response—

And now for a moment the sun comes out, on this
         journey that is part of a farther voyage still
(Long, long after Magellan)
With the home port long since forgotten, and the
         ultimate reaches not even guessed—

Then a flurry of snow, and after that night, and the last
         stop
(It is the ten thousandth trip, but no band is playing;
         there had been no champagne at the first)
The driver simply reverses his illumined signs,
Singly, the passengers descend and resume, resume their
         separate ways—

Disillusioned (and used to it), alone and self-absorbed,
Unaware that Sinbad the Sailor has descended with
         them, and that Cyclops, Cinderella, the Princess
         of the Diamond Isles in love with Captain
         Wonder,
And Jack the Giant Killer have all been companions of
         theirs—

And that each of these has still a long, much longer way
         to go.

Family Album (1)

The Pioneers

They lived with dangers they alone could see,
Aware of them, everywhere and always, with X-ray eyes
    for the graver and subtle risks of impending evil
    and future guilt,
Sorcerers of the newsroom, genii of the wide screen,
    brevet phrenologists of bureau, cabinet, and
    court,
Consultant wizards of the high, the low, and the middle
    mirage—

Our forbears, quaint and queer in these posed
    photographs, stiffly smiling, no hint of their
    martyrdom revealed,
(But for the diaries they commissioned, we would not
    know their heartaches, even now)—

Visionaries (but practical), when the guilty fled in long
    black limousines,
Found clever refuge in opera boxes, night clubs, art
    galleries and public parks,
Our elders pursued in 300 horsepower sportscars,
    disguised as playboys, undercover girls,

If the crisis required it, posed successfully as double or
     triple agents, maniacs, drunks—

For thus they freed that raw, mid-century chaos of little
     empires from the pestilence of false thought;
Helped write, and signed, so many of the Magna Cartas
     in use to this very day;
Issued the first crude registry of licenced Truth;
Sought (and received) patents for the better types of
     logic, durable humour, authentic taste;
Chartered the standard modes of legal prayer, for lease
     on a yearly basis,
(Renewable, with the forms filled in and the stamps
     affixed, for a nominal fee;
This trifling charge scarcely covers the cost;
What matters, of course, is the thought)—

God sometimes spoke to them on sleepless nights (as
     they told us, often), and they took down every
     word,
Revised and edited the counsel in the morning, making
     sure the names and addresses were correct,
Then gave it to the world, stamped: *For Immediate
     Release*—

They were not Gods, nor did they claim to be;
They were human, and fallible, content to be just what
     they were:
God's public relations.

Family Album (2)

Granny

This is Grandmother Susan, in one of the few pictures
       taken by the press,
(*Think!* published this one, and here Grandma is leaving
       court, perhaps to gather evidence for the next
       case)
She is twenty-five, here, in a frock typical of those
       innocent but turbulent times,
And we cannot tell, from the picture, whether she is
       armed—

Armed and equipped to perfection with the weapon she
       gave the sorcery of her special art,
The recorder snuggled in its holster, the holster
       concealed in her handbag, her girdle, sometimes
       her brassiere,
(With the listening microphone hidden—where?
The guilty, for all their cunning, never dreamed)
While the steadily turning reels, winding in compact
       silence, caught every guilty nuance of every
       guilty phrase,
("How about it, babe?" reorganized Chemosene; a drug
       firm failed on a whisper)
Stored away the convincing background noise of ice in
       shakers, the sound of authentic laughter,
And trapped, beyond reasonable doubt, the blackest
       crimes ever committed in speech—

While Granny smiled and dimpled in sympathy:
"Hi-Fi Sue Scores Again,"
"*Think!* names this average, all-round girl America's
      sweetheart of the year"—

Though there were rumours, and slanders, and yes,
      many jokes;
Grandpa, they said, was a deafmute—

But where are these jokers now?

Family Album (3)

The Boat

Our scholars say of this latest find, the boat uncovered
      in the desert sands,
Distant from templed places, far from trade routes,
      remote from the sea,
(But seaworthy, preserved in its arid tomb, still perfect
      in every wrought detail)—

They claim that this one, too, is a funeral vessel,
      designed for passage throughout the farthest
      islands in the sky of death,
Not a landlocked memorial, merely, bound nowhere,
But a solar craft on phantom course (as the helm is
      fixed) for the royal ports of the Ptolemaic year,
Bearing the illustrious dead, in safety, everywhere about
      that planned and prudent empire of the dead,

Under orders sealed by monarchs centuries before, on
        errands of state the dead must observe—

And this accords, it is true, with the intricate innocence
        of that age,
For they reveled, as we know, in matters that were
        skilfully and lucidly deranged—

But some of our savants claim this boat is of later
        origin—indeed, very late;
These say it derives from a wholly different rite;
This bark, they say, was a test and trial of the atom's
        might as related, mystically, to the actual sea;
That the Idaho ship is not pagan, at all, and differs, in
        many ways, from that early vessel of the Nile.

Family Album (4)

The Investigators

WHO DO YOU, WHO DO YOU, WHO DO YOU, WHO?
WHO DO YOU KNOW, WHO DO YOU HEAR ABOUT, WHO
        DO YOU SEE AND MEET IN YOUR DREAMS AND
        DAYDREAMS?—

Look what we found when we almost caught him, and
        he nearly confessed again and again,
Stacks and heaps of flagons and flasks and tubes and
        coils,

"Secret" it says on the door,
(Whatever that means, whoever lost it here, or threw it
   away, or he just forgot)
Crystals and powders and serums and herbs, who's got a
   hairpin,
Where's a corkscrew,
How would the blue stuff go with a gallon of green?—

WHO, WHO WHO?
WHAT WERE YOU WHEN, WHY WERE YOU WHAT, WHERE
   WERE YOU WHICH, EITHER HOW OR WHY?

Could it be, no doubt an alchemist lived here once,
(Whoever knows how, it's easy to transmute lead into
   pure, solid, genuine gold)
But why does it look so tasty,
Perhaps you don't rub it on, you drink it instead,
It must be the essence of eternal youth and truth, beauty
   and health and duty and wealth,
Or at least second sight,
What are we waiting for, how will we ever find out until
   somebody tries?—

WHERE DO YOU, WHEN DO YOU?
HOW DO YOU WHICH?
WHO'S IN IT FOR WHAT, WHAT'S IN IT FOR WHO?—

Close your eyes tight, turn around three times, reach
   and pour and stir,
(It says in the rules, one wish per man)

Whatever it is, this is bound to be something final and
      big,
Open the valve, who's got a match?—

HOW DO YOU, WHEN DO YOU, WHERE DO YOU WHAT?
WHO DO YOU WHO, WHO DO YOU WHO, WHO DO YOU
      WHO?

BIOGRAPHICAL NOTE

Kenneth Fearing was born in Oak Park, Illinois, on July 28, 1902. His father was a lawyer. After his parents divorced, he was raised by an aunt. He graduated from Oak Park–River Forest High School and enrolled at the University of Illinois in 1920, then transferred to the University of Wisconsin, where he contributed to the *Wisconsin Literary Magazine* as one of its editors. After receiving a B.A. from Wisconsin in 1924, he moved to Chicago briefly and then to New York City, where he began to publish pulp fiction under pseudonyms. Late in the 1920s his poetry began appearing regularly, particularly in left-wing magazines such as *Partisan Review* and *New Masses*. His first poetry collection, *Angel Arms*, was published in 1929. He was awarded Guggenheim Fellowships in 1936 and in 1939. In addition to seven volumes of poetry, he wrote several novels, including *Clark Gifford's Body* (1942) and *The Big Clock* (1948). In the 1940s and 50s he contributed to *The New York Times Book Review*. He worked at *Newsweek* from 1952 to 1954 and as a publicist for the Muscular Dystrophy Association from 1955 to 1958. He was married twice and was the father of a son. He died in New York City on June 26, 1961.

The texts of the poems in this volume are printed as they first appeared in one of Kenneth Fearing's seven collections: *Angel Arms* (New York: Coward McCann, 1929); *Poems* (New York: Dynamo, 1935); *Dead Reckoning* (New York: Random House, 1938); *Collected Poems* (New York: Random House, 1940); *Afternoon of a Pawnbroker and Other Poems* (New York: Harcourt, Brace and Company, 1943); *Stranger at Coney Island and Other Poems* (New York: Harcourt, Brace and Company, 1948); and *New and Selected Poems* (Bloomington: Indiana University Press, 1956). Although Fearing revised many of the poems from the 1930s for publication in *Collected Poems*, the earlier book versions are printed here because the chronological arrangement of the present volume is intended to emphasize his development as a poet. Poems taken from *Collected Poems* and *New and Selected Poems*, such as the selections from "The Agency" and "Family Album" sequences, first appeared in book form in these collections.

This volume presents the texts of the original printings chosen for inclusion here, but it does not attempt to reproduce nontextual features of their typographic design. The texts are presented without change, except for the correction of typographical errors. Spelling, punctuation, and capitalization are often expressive features and are not altered, even when inconsistent or irregular. The following is a list of typographical errors corrected, cited by page and line number: 38.9, sybils; 53.8, heart-to heart; 55.14, lavendar; 61.1, Denoument; 61.22, denoument; 66.27, leading; 133.8, Seer's.

NOTES

6.4   Max Nordau]   Hungarian physician, cultural critic, and Zionist leader (1849–1923) whose *Degeneration* (1895) was widely influential.

36.6   Gene Tunney]   American boxer (1897–1978), heavyweight champion from 1926 to 1928.

36.6   Will Hays]   From 1922 to 1945 Hays (1879–1954) was head of the Motion Picture Producers and Distributors of America, often called the "Hays office." In 1930 the MPPDA adopted a production code regulating the moral content of movies, which remained in effect until 1966.

42.11   RFC]   The Reconstruction Finance Corporation, established by Congress in 1932, made loans to businesses, industries, and banks.

44.10   Beatrice Fairfax]   Pseudonym of a syndicated advice columnist.

44.11   *Father Coughlin*]   Charles Coughlin (1891–1979), Catholic priest and popular radio broadcaster during the 1930s. He initially supported the New Deal but then turned against Franklin Roosevelt and in 1938 began making anti-Semitic and pro-fascist statements in his broadcasts.

44.11–12   *Miss Aimee Semple McPherson*]   McPherson (1890–1944), also known as "Sister Aimee," was a Los Angeles–based radio evangelist and founder, in 1927, of the International Church of the Foursquare Gospel.

44.12   *General Hugh Johnson*] After his retirement from the army Brigadier General Hugh S. Johnson (1882–1942) wrote a widely read newspaper column. He was appointed head of the National Recovery Administration by Roosevelt in 1933.

44.13   *Barbara Mdivani*] Heiress to the Woolworth fortune Barbara Hutton (1912–1979). The Georgian prince Alexis Mdivani was the first of her seven husbands.

44.13   *Samuel Insull*] English-born financier (1859–1938) whose enormous public-utilities empire in America collapsed in 1932. Insull fled the country but was extradited in 1934 on fraud and embezzlement charges, of which he was acquitted.

44.14   *Mr. Prince Mike Romanoff*] "Prince Mike" was the nickname given to Harry Gerguson, a Lithuanian immigrant and con man who attempted to pass himself off as Prince Michael Romanoff, cousin of the late Russian czar.

47.21   Lydia Pinkham] The herbal medicines patented by Lydia Estes Pinkham (1819–1883) were popular treatments for the alleviation of women's ailments.

50.9   Bowie] Maryland racetrack.

83.2   I am . . . Hague] Democratic Party boss Frank Hague (1876–1956) served eight terms as mayor of Jersey City, NJ; he made his most notorious remark, "I am the law!," in a 1937 speech.

96.8   Krueger-Musica denouement] After his suicide in 1932 the Swedish magnate Ivar Krueger, known as the "Match King," was found to have defrauded investors of millions. Using the alias F. Donald Coster, the con man Philip Musica headed the drug company McKesson & Robbins and used his position to embezzle money and engage in other illegal activities; he shot himself just as police were about to arrest him at his home in Fairfield, Connecticut, on December 16, 1938.

138.15   Martin Dies] Texas congressman Martin Dies (1901–1972) served as the first chairman of the House Un-American Activities Committee from 1938 to 1945.

INDEX OF TITLES AND FIRST LINES